Elvis' Secret Legacy

Cherry McKenzie

Bloomington, IN   Milton Keynes, UK

authorHOUSE™

AuthorHouse™
1663 Liberty Drive, Suite 200
Bloomington, IN 47403
www.authorhouse.com
Phone: 1-800-839-8640

AuthorHouse™ UK Ltd.
500 Avebury Boulevard
Central Milton Keynes, MK9 2BE
www.authorhouse.co.uk
Phone: 08001974150

This book is a work of fiction. People, places, events, and situations are the product of the author's imagination. Any resemblance to actual persons, living or dead, or historical events, is purely coincidental.

First published by AuthorHouse 10/12/2006

ISBN: 1-4259-4114-1 (sc)

Printed in the United States of America
Bloomington, Indiana

This book is printed on acid-free paper.

Acknowledgments

First I would like to thank my family—my daughters Melanie Ferrari, Cindy McKenzie and Michele Teske for their enthusiastic belief that my creativity would actually take finished form (a gold star to Michele for her editing); my granddaughter Savannah Rose Senko for the great happiness and love she inspires; my sister Pamela Worrell for her insightful suggestions and contagious joy of life and my son-in-law Don Ferrari for his helpful ideas.

I am indebted to my dear long time friend Mary Estell Page for the earliest manuscript critique and relentless encouragement that would not allow me to stop. Her mountainside home in the Kiamiche Wilderness provided a magical place to commune with my muse.

My appreciation goes to Helen Widner for her direction and valuable information.

Special thanks to Barbara Weatherly Rice for the photos in the back. She is seated on the left in the picture. Barbara emailed these remembrances:

"God, dust off my brain: If I remember correctly you were at Humes for a short time when Presley asked you out. He was nice to you the whole time. You looked so pretty that night. Always had a sweet smile. I sang at the Prom. I was singing with a band named Bob Bevington. For some reason, I couldn't remember the words to You Belong To Me and had to read the words off a card. The guy I went with was named Hugh. Came in a cab and brought me a lovely corsage. Ironic! I was singing here and there and the quiet one that sat across from me turned out to be an icon."

Chapter One

A trio of white meditation candles glowed amid scattered crystals on the makeshift altar atop the antique chest of drawers. Phantom figures flickered along the wall as Kat McBride laid on her bed. Out of nowhere his midsouth drawl suddenly whispered into the nape of her neck. The voice asked a favor.

On the evening of August sixteenth, Kat McBride slipped the new creativity tape into the player. She took a deep breath and following the instructions stretched out full length on her bed. She felt lean and tall. Taller than her five and a half feet. The fifteen yo-yo pounds had disappeared in the weeks after her cosmetic surgery along with her appetite. The newly tightened skin against her high cheek bones reveal an almost beautiful face framed by short curly blonde hair. Now that her exterior was healing nicely it was time to concentrate on her interior. A little spiritual fine-tuning.

The monotone voice of the speakers invited her. "Imagine yourself on a beautiful sandy beach. It's sunset. The palm trees are blowing gently in the tropical breeze as you take three deep breaths...and completely relax."

She breathed in and out slowly---the room began to slip away. On her third exhale, he spoke for the first time. "Kitty, I need a favor." The voice sounded familiar and she knew it came from Memphis. That's the only place anyone still called her Kitty.

Kitty, pussy, cat calls. Bad jokes. She had left that name behind years ago when she married Bobby Joe. He liked to call her Kat and she liked the idea of starting her new life with a completely new name. Her last name had changed a couple of times over the years but she had liked McBride and always returned to it.

Kat McBride.

Permanently. Maybe.

The voice continued. "Honey, I don't care what you call yourself now. I need your help." Then he appeared, walking beside her on the sandy beach of her visualized paradise.

Elvis Presley!

He could have stepped out of a page in the Humes High School yearbook. Or Miss Helen Lochrie's speech and drama class. He'd always stood out among the crew cuts. Long sideburns. Dark brown hair brushed back on the sides into a D.A. She smiled, remembering that long ago hairstyle that resembled a duck's ass when it came together in the back.

And he definitely dressed to his own bizarre drummer. This outfit was conservative. White tuxedo dress shirt with the top two buttons left open. Long sleeves rolled a couple of turns. Collar flipped up. Black slacks. No shoes. No footprints.

Wait a minute!

She took another deep breath, closed her eyes and channeled all her energy into banishing Elvis.

"Go away," she silently commanded.

The complete vision abruptly vanished.

"No! Just Elvis! For heaven sake! I'm trying to meditate."

Out of the blackness, at the exact mid point, high on the back of her neck, he whispered to her. "I'm sorry darlin', but this is way too important. I'll be back."

Chapter Two

The sun seeped in through the slits in the blinds putting an end to the perplexing night. Kat glanced with disgust at the blank pages of her open journal on the bed beside her. The more she had attempted to record the bizarre happenings, the more elusive her thoughts. Her recollections flashed on and off like a malfunctioning movie projector.

Did yesterday's date have anything to do with her manifestation? August sixteenth. A day of mourning for all Elvis fans. Could the concentrated grieving and remembering of his death by so many people somehow distort her meditation?

She hadn't experienced a conscious thought of Elvis in a very long time. Why would she be contacted by his spirit now? Or why hallucinate about him? The answer nagged like a memory struggling to resurface. Kat tried to reassure herself. It was a figment, an illusion or blockage from Ego to knock her off her spiritual path.

She had taken a few months off from her real estate business to devote herself to a vision quest of sorts. A soul search. An inner journey. Besides Bobby Joe couldn't stand the idea of her getting older and had offered to pay for a face-lift. Taking money from him had never been a problem. They seemed to circle back to each other whenever they were simultaneously between romances. He'd always been generous with his money and she had always been receptive. Guilt put him in a giving mood and Kat was a great guilt giver.

After all, he had ended up with the business they had started. The small glass shop had grown into a huge supplier of commercial glass and now had a separate windshield department that catered to the car repair industry.

He always said if she hadn't been there in the beginning he would never have had the guts to go into business for himself. Of course he was drunk when he said it---a fairly regular occurrence. Kat seconded that opinion anyway.

Now, with a brand new face she could concentrate on polishing her inner self. Take spiritual retreats.

Meditate more.

However during the next week she became so busy that she really didn't have time to meditate. Every time she would start to put in a tape she'd remember a drawer that needed to be cleaned. Or a friend she hadn't called in a while. The house had never been so spotless and she had not talked to so many old friends in years.

On the other hand, sleep was elusive so she would read until she dropped off...or watch old movies. Always consuming several glasses of wine in the process.

The nights grew longer as the glasses of wine got bigger until one evening finally stretched all the way to dawn.

"This is ridiculous," she muttered, struggling to remain situated on the side of the bed. "Pretty soon I'll be having wine with my oatmeal."

She definitely needed some inner direction. Kat walked determinedly toward the drawer where she kept her all occasion tapes and began flipping through them. Motivation. Meditation. Relaxation. Stimulation. Stop smoking. Start Dieting. Serenity. Enthusiasm. Private Passion. Public Speaking. Self help tapes. She had accumulated quite a collection over the years.

Kat rejected the beaches with the sound of seagulls and gently rolling waves in favor of the Tibetan monks chanting in accompaniment to the ancient mystical harmony of hollow cane wind chimes.

Actually she liked the guided imagery that most of her tapes contained. However, she felt a real departure was needed. Maybe she could empty her mind, meditate and contact her spirit guide, Herald. She wasn't positive he existed but naming him brought her a strange kind of comfort. He listened when she talked.

Kat stretched out on her bed and started the countdown from twenty to one. She began drifting to the calming cadence of the chants, together with the soothing echo of the bamboo chimes. She thought of her toes, loosening their tension to the ancient tempo and then continued climbing upward through her feet and legs finally liberating her back and shoulders. Sleep almost captured her as the softening relaxation drifted toward her head.

"Can't say I like your new taste in music, darling."

Her body stiffened. Eyes flashed open. She was instantly alert. The room was empty of course.

"I can materialize if you want me to," said the familiar voice. "It takes some effort and I haven't done it often, but I can give it a shot."

Kat screamed "No!" as she bolted upright in the bed. A minute passed. The only sounds in the room were the monks and the reverberating wind chimes.

Sleep deprivation. I'm hearing voices, Kat thought. No, only one voice. His. But why? Kat needed advice. Something strange was happening.

Chapter Three

The shabby Mexican restaurant was almost empty when Kat walked in. It was cool, dark and decorated with cheap manufactured folk art. She stood at the entrance still squinting from the sun, and searched the booths and tables for her best friend and fellow explorer into the paranormal.

Posey Street and Kat had known each other for more than a dozen years. They had met while attending a workshop on auras and angels. Immediate soul sisters.

Work kept them from seeing each other daily. The phone and email were their regular means of contact. However, they took their vacations and weekend retreats together. They were both members of the North Texas Paranormal Club and generally had drinks after the monthly meeting. Kat felt this situation was too bizarre to hash over in an email or fifteen-minute phone conversation. She definitely needed more input. Posey's logical Virgo nature could been counted on to give down-to-earth advice.

Kat spotted Posey in a back booth next to an enormous fake cactus draped with red pepper twinkle lights. She hurried toward her.

Posey was taller than Kat with the slender grace of a once upon-time-dancer. She emphasized a gypsy quality in the bohemian way she dressed. Bold colors, bright jewelry with hair a little long and wild.

"You look better than I thought you would," Posey observed. "Not quite six weeks out of surgery. I'm surprised your makeup could cover up so much. And not a dark root showing. I'm impressed."

"You know I'm a natural blonde." Kat countered as she slipped into the booth opposite Posey.

"I know Natural Blonde is the color you use."

"And you use Dark Chocolate Brown to match your eyes. I think we should be grateful that neither of us has started using blue yet." Kat pointed to the barely noticeable bruises under each eye. "I look like the loser in a domestic dispute, but I'm not likely to run into anyone I know in this charming establishment. I had a hard time finding it myself. Do you think we should have lunch here?"

Posey smiled. "You said you wanted an out-of-the-way place. This was the most far out place I could think of. Doesn't it make you nostalgic for some of the picturesque cantinas we frequented in Mexico?"

"After an afternoon of margaritas, more than the drinks were blended. The cantinas blurred into a one look fits all."

"Well as far as lunch is concerned, I'm not even sure we should drink the water. That's why I ordered a beer."

"A little early isn't it?"

"It's happy hour somewhere. Want one?"

Kat held up two fingers to the waiter headed in their direction. He nodded and disappeared back into the kitchen.

"Besides," Posey continued, "I can't remember the last time you've wanted to have lunch with me during the week. Plus, you're too vain to make a public appearance so soon after surgery unless it's really important. You wouldn't even let me come to see you. I decided I might need to be fortified for something this earth-shaking. What's the mystery problem?"

Kat took a deep breath, closed her eyes. Where to begin?

Finally she blurted out, "It's Elvis!"

"I beg your pardon? In your condition you've managed to meet a guy named Elvis?" Posey shook her head in amazement.

"I knew you couldn't stay alone too much longer, but this is fast even for you. A doctor? Male nurse? What?"

"No! The Elvis!" Kat whispered as the waiter approached with the beers.

They waited in silence until he was out of earshot.

"As in Presley?" Posey's dark coffee eyes beamed with awakening interest. She leaned forward. "Sounds intriguing. Tell me more."

Kat started with the first apparition and thirty minutes later concluded with Elvis' promise to return.

Posey listened intently as she absently toyed with the wisp of dark hair that had escaped her carelessly upswept hairdo.

After a brief silence she spoke. "I think you should go on the assumption that this is a valid visitation. It can't hurt to err on the side of preparation. After all, he's not a stranger. You did go to a prom together."

Chapter Four

During the drive home Kat mulled over her conversation with Posey. They had both ruled out demonic possession. However, Kat decided she'd wear the gold-plated cross the Spaniard had given her for their first and only wedding anniversary. A little extra protection couldn't hurt.

She already did the white light bit. She never began a meditation without first mentally surrounding herself with it. Well, maybe not always. But she generally remembered to before she fell asleep.

Posey's mention of the 1952 Humes High School junior/ senior prom had flooded her senses with bits and pieces of memories. Her thoughts returned to those perplexing, puzzling, euphoric days. The highs and lows of the first hormonal imbalance.

Elvis had waited on the stairwell between classes to invite her to the dance, with the unbelievable promise that if she would go with him on such short notice he would never bother her again. A promise she would help him break only once.

She had transferred to Humes the month before from Southside High and now it was only a week until the prom. Not much time to find the perfect dress.

However she and her mother immediately began the quest. She missed a whole day of school so that they could go downtown to explore the department stores and fancy boutiques.

They found it on a mannequin in the window of a small shop. A ballerina length, strapless, lilac taffeta creation with matching net overlay and stole. Mother had even let her borrow her expensive gold and amethyst necklace and earrings.

The molasses-moving week shifted into swift current when THE DAY arrived. How her heart had skipped at the sound of the doorbell. When she opened the door, Elvis stood there, wearing a dark blue suit and a half smile, upper lip slightly curled. A tantalizing full smile enveloped his face as he handed her the corsage box.

"I asked the lady at the flower shop what would be the best thing to get you. I never bought flowers before."

An orchid! Her first to receive; his first to give. She'd kept it even after all that was left was the ribbon. She still had it.

His old gray car (with the rust hole in the floor board covered by a black rubber mat) was parked on the street in front of the house. When he opened her door and she slipped inside, it became a brand new, next century ride. They glided to the hotel.

Traditionally the ballroom was decorated by the juniors in honor of the seniors. This year, was as usual, a mass of Humes' colors. Orange and white streamers cascaded from the ceiling over the dance floor. An enormous arch of orange and white balloons decorated one end of the room. Each table had a duo of the same balloons floating upward with streamers tied to a ceramic tiger, the school mascot.

She and Elvis danced every slow dance, his cheek lightly touching the top of her head, while his arms held her softly against him. However, when the tempo picked up, Elvis would lead her back to their seats. He was too shy to try the fast music because he said he had never learned the right steps. But by the way his body moved to the rhythm while they listened, Kat knew that his feet would have found a way.

Too soon, the familiar "Stardust" melody mingled with the turning mirrored ball high above the dance floor to create a magical final dance. The enchantment lingered through the ride home.

Her most vivid recollection was the return to her front door. What a sweet tender mouth he had. It still filled her with awe that he had asked permission to kiss her goodnight. In all her life he was the only person to ever do that.

The thought of being with him again was appealing; if she could just be sure it was really Elvis trying to contact her.

Whatever was happening, she had to face it. Even if it meant that she really was having a nervous breakdown.

Tonight she would put out her crystals, light the candles, burn the incense, put on harp music and wait.

Chapter Five

Kat simply could not relax. Tension began in her head, extended through her neck then hardened her shoulders as she lay on her bed. Hesitantly she peered through her dark lashes. Eerie shapes wafted across the bedroom wall as the aromatic candle scented the air with sandalwood. It had been at least thirty minutes since she had carefully set the stage for Elvis' return.

A no-show.

Well, she hadn't really expected him. It wasn't as if he'd stood her up. Her attitude had turned off more than one man. She doubted that spirits were immune. Besides he may have had other houses to haunt. Surely she couldn't be the only one who could help him with his problem. Whatever that might be....

Kat felt a little silly as she washed the make up off her face, and then slipped out of the seductive black gown that she hadn't worn since her last honeymoon. She went to the dresser and pulled out her favorite nightshirt. It was so worn the message on the front was barely visible. The faded red letters proclaimed "If I'm so spiritual why do I stay pissed all the time?"

"How appropriate," she thought as she pulled it over her head.

"I liked the other outfit better."

Kat whirled around in the direction of the voice. There he was, lying on the bed. Well he wasn't quite all there. Just enough to make him out. Kat could still see the floral design in the quilt pattern where he was kind of hovering.

She closed her eyes then opened them slowly.

Still hovering.

"I apologize for my condition," Elvis continued. "I know I look kind of faded. Can't seem to get all the vibrations going in the right direction. It would help if I could get a little positive energy from you."

Kat's mind was tumbling around in all directions. Speech was out of the question so she mutely stared at the transparent figure.

"I know it must be a shock for me to just show up after all these years. But it's like I told you before, I need your help."

Transfixed, Kat managed to sputter, " Wha, what do you want?"

"Well darlin', you may have read that the last years of my life weren't exactly without complications. I was in... How can I put this? An altered state of awareness a lot of the time."

"You were on drugs," Kat stated flatly.

Elvis smiled.

"Prescription drugs. It just sort of slipped up on me. Kind of blurred my perspective. That's one of the bad things about dying. You get a complete review of your life through crystal clear memory." Elvis paused, and then laughed.

"It's Hell!" He shook his head, while taking a deep somber breath. "But back to why I'm here. There's one foolish thing I did that you can help me undo."

Kat felt the mesmerizing intensity in his eyes before he continued.

"I need you to help me rob a bank."

"You're out of your mind," Kat snapped.

Elvis grinned. "No, I still have my mind. It's a body I'm lacking."

"You don't need money where you are," Kat declared.

"It's not that kind of bank. It's a sperm bank. I made a deposit I'd like to withdraw."

"A sperm bank?" Kat repeated incredulously.

"Yeah. I had this idea that I'd like to reincarnate back into myself. I knew I'd really messed up this time and I wanted another shot at it."

"That's not how it works," Kat replied quickly.

"I know that now, darlin'. I told you my thinking got pretty fuzzy toward the end. Anyway, as long as that little glob of protein stayed frozen, it wasn't hurting anybody."

"Now somebody is going to thaw it out?" Kat asked.

"And fertilize," Elvis finished.

Kat raised her hand in a stop gesture. "Wait a minute. This is all going too fast for me. How can I be sure I'm not just hallucinating? That I didn't just conjure you up? You could be just a manifestation of my imagination. I've been known to create some really bizarre fantasies."

Elvis began to rise and drift toward her.

"Stop," Kat commanded as she backed toward the door.

Too late. Elvis was miraculously within kissing distance.

"Kitty, sweetness, I'm not your imagination," Elvis whispered soothingly. "Look into my eyes and you'll know the truth."

Reluctantly Kat met the endless depth of his gaze. The room seemed to breathe with a dazzling white light that wrapped around them, merging them into one entity. They pulsated to the rhythm of a single heart beat. Every cell in her body vibrated to some distant melody.

Then the music could be heard. Elvis was singing, "When we kissed my heart's on fire, burning with a strange desire. So my darling please, surrender...

Kat was ready to surrender anything. Believe anything.

Chapter Six

"You weren't home last night," Kat announced as she hurried through the door of Posey's metaphysical bookstore, The Cosmos.

"Or this morning," she continued as she approached Posey restocking a bookshelf.

"You're not the only one with a sex life," Posey retorted. "Granted mine is not quite as active or diverse as yours, but it does exist."

"Very funny. So don't tell me where you were."

"I won't," Posey answered cheerfully.

Kat glanced around the small shop then motioned toward the closed door of the stockroom.

"Are we alone?" she whispered.

"Yeah. Mary is at the dentist until later this afternoon. What's going on? You look like you've seen a ghost," Posey teased.

"I did see him. Last night. He materialized right there on my bed."

"On your bed?" Why am I not surprised?" Posey replied.

"Be serious," Kat pleaded. "I need your help. We've got to go to Memphis."

"We? To Memphis?" Posey questioned.

"Yes, we've got to rob a sperm bank."

"Halt, right there!" Posey shook her head in astonishment as she hurried toward the front door. She quickly turned the "Closed" sign facing the outside.

"Let's go in the back room for a cup of tea and a little chat."

"Oh, come on Posey." Kat implored. "You've always wanted to go on a ghost tour. How could you pass up the opportunity to have a spirit travel with you? It will be an adventure."

Chapter Seven

Kat's new maroon Lincoln Town Car zoomed onto the old Memphis Bridge. Across the way the new bridge sparkled in the early evening twilight.

"That's a pretty sight. Looks like it's decorated for Christmas with white twinkle lights," Posey observed.

"I don't think I'll ever feel comfortable driving on it. This one is like an old friend. Once I start across I know I'm really home," Kat replied.

"I'm real glad you took the old bridge. Hope you girls don't mind but I thought I'd ride in with you," came a voice from the back.

"Mind! I was beginning to wonder if you were ever going to show up," Kat replied as she shot a quick look behind her.

Sure enough, there was Elvis lounging in the approximate vicinity of the rear passenger area.

"I hope that wasn't Elvis you were talking to. Please tell me you were just thinking out loud," Posey implored.

"Oh god! You can't hear him? Look in the back seat. Can you see anything?"

Posey shifted around to face the back.

"Nothing."

"Squint your eyes," Kat demanded.

"Somehow I don't think this is going to work," Posey said as she followed instructions.

"Nope. Nothing but an eighteen wheeler with bright lights about to ride your back end."

"I don't believe this," Kat shouted, as she shot Elvis a furious look in the rearview mirror. "You promised that you would explain everything to her yourself. That's the only way I got her to come on this stupid trip. How are you going to explain anything if she can't see or hear you?"

"Easy darlin'. Turn on the radio."

"Any particular station?" Kat quipped, sarcastically.

"Would you mind sharing with me exactly what's going on here?" Posey asked, as she studied her friend in the bright lights of the truck edging closer to their back bumper.

"He wants me to turn on the radio," Kat snapped.

"Mood music?" Posey guessed.

"I have no idea."

"Let's humor him," Posey suggested. She switched on the radio. Mostly static with bits of unidentifiable music burst forth before Posey adjusted the noise level down.

"I wish that trucker would quit crowding. He's beginning to make me nervous," Kat fumed.

"He could be the one you were flirting with at that truck stop. He probably just wants your phone number. Guess he didn't see my "for a good time" message on the men's restroom door."

Kat gave her friend a fake smile as she reached down and snapped off the radio.

"That static is driving me crazy. Elvis will just have to wait until we're out of traffic."

The enormous refrigerator truck finally switched to the left lane just as Kat veered to the right onto highway 55. The driver honked his horn as he passed.

"Maybe he did get your message."

"If he passes it on to his buddies you may get to be real popular."

"Don't worry. I'll share," Kat retorted.

"I can see we're not going to get anywhere until we can find a quiet place where we can be alone. It'll be easier for me to channel my vibrations," Elvis interjected.

"She can't see you. She can't hear you. Your solution is to turn on the radio and you expect me to remain calm while driving with a megaton truck breathing down my neck."

"Obviously that was way too much to ask. Just pull into Riverside Park when you come to it," Elvis advised soothingly.

"Now I know you're from another dimension. If we go into that park at night, we're going to get mugged or worse. Not to mention that it's probably illegal."

"Nothing is going to happen," Elvis replied calmly.

"Not to you. You're already dead!" Kat retaliated.

"Excuse me! I vote no on the park. And if you don't start giving me an "as it happens" update, I'm jumping out of the car the next time you stop and finding a cab to the airport," Posey stated emphatically.

Kat gave her friend a look of total frustration. Her emotions were in such a tangle, her mind racing in every direction. Coherent conversation was hopeless. They continued down the road in awkward silence.

"Here! Turn off here!" Elvis suddenly commanded.

"I don't believe I just did that," Kat exclaimed as she drove down the Mallory Road Exit.

"I don't believe you just did that either. Maybe it's time to stop taking orders from the other side."

"Good heavens! There's a dead end sign, "Kat shouted as she slowed the car. "Is that some kind of factory behind that fence?"

"I can't tell what those big black shapes are, but I'd just as soon try to figure them out in the rearview mirror. Let's hope there's a place to turn around."

"Calm down girls. That's just the old Delta Oil refinery. Besides we're going to make a right hand turn...now."

The car immediately responded by entering the shadowy darkness of vine tangled trees that created an eerie arch at the park's entrance.

"Wait a minute! I voted no on the park issue," Posey shouted.

The machine seemed to have private energy as it picked up speed while traveling the narrow twisting roads into the park's interior. Kat and Posey exchanged looks of horror as they mutually realized their lack of control. The car continued at a steady pace until it rounded a curve and came upon a clearing. Kat felt her foot press downward on the brake until the Lincoln glided into a smooth stop on a bluff over looking the Mississippi River.

The Bluff.

She had watched her share of submarine races from this very spot. The last one had been spectacular.

"Bring back some memories?" Elvis asked tenderly.

Kat's eyes brimmed with tears as she tried to swallow the emotions caught in her throat. Oh yes, indeed she remembered.

"Was I ever that young or naive?" Kat asked wistfully.

"We both were," Elvis answered.

Posey sensed the new vibrations in the air as she studied her friend by the moonlight that filtered through the windshield. Finally she spoke.

"Don't tell me that harrowing ride we just took was down Memory Lane."

Kat turned and gave her friend a pensive smile. Before she could speak, Elvis did.

"Okay, sweetheart, it's time to go to work," He instructed softly. "Turn the radio on, and then twist the dial to that fuzzy area between stations."

Kat obediently did as she was told, as Posey watched in amused silence.

Suddenly the famous voice seemed to wrap itself around the static, emerging out the speakers, giving the tone a stereophonic sound within the car interior.

"I think Posey can hear me now. Is that right, darlin'?" Elvis continued, addressing Posey for the first time.

Kat turned to her friend for confirmation. Posey's face seemed frozen into a wide-eyed mask of total amazement.

"You look as if you'd just heard a ghost!" Kat collapsed with relief into uncontrollable laughter

Chapter Eight

In daylight, Elvis Presley Boulevard was not a pretty sight. Kat and Posey had driven down it the evening before in search of a motel. Darkness and neon had masked its commercial ugliness.

The shattering glare of a midsouth early September morning dissolved the veil of any lingering illusions. Battered businesses, in varying stages of beginnings to endings, spread boundless around them. A pawn shop, business school, a number of multi–cultural restaurants, fast food chains, gas stations- all mixed haphazardly with the predominate form of commerce- cars. All kinds of cars. Dealerships of every type. Each appeared to have its own used car lot.

"This place has a real greedy, worn feel to it," Posey observed while waiting for Kat to unlock the car doors.

"It's definitely the place to come if you're looking for a new or used auto. Wonder why they all located out here?" Kat reflected.

"Maybe Elvis' car museum puts them in the mood," Posey jested as she slipped into the passenger seat.

"It's hard to believe that all of this was once considered the outskirts of Memphis. Elvis wasn't the only one keeping horses back then," Kat said as she turned and smiled. "Are you ready for the radio?"

"Sure, maybe he's changed his mind. I still can't believe they didn't have one in the room."

"I'd have settled for a TV that worked. Fixing it today is a little late for our entertainment. However, Elvis is right to wait so we can hear the plans together and one step at a time. That way we won't get confused."

"I passed confusion a long time ago. This as a karmic debt I have to pay. Sure hope the pleasure was worth the possible price," Posey lamented.

"Whatever our past, I'll bet we shared the mischief. Why else would we have the same karmic pay back now?," Kat countered playfully.

"Maybe to cancel out some of the trespasses we're accumulating this lifetime," Posey speculated.

Kat's eyes twinkled. "Oh, I'm sure we've been a lot naughtier in some other incarnation. At least I hope so."

Posey returned her smile." Before this trip is over we'll know just how bad we've been. Somehow I'm hoping we didn't have too much fun. Oh hell, turn on the radio. Might as well face the music."

"Perhaps Elvis will sing for us," Kat laughed as she switched on the dial.

"Mornin' ladies. What song would you like to hear? Can't imagine a better way to start the day than serenading two lovely ladies. By the way Posey, how's the reception?"

"The audio is great. I just wish I had a place to focus." Posey narrowed her eyes as she turned toward the back seat. "Nothing yet."

"I'm working on it. We just have to get our vibrations more in tune. You can still see me all right can't you Kitty?"

"Yeah, I can see you. But since you're working on reception, can you make yourself a few years older? Your appearance is a little disconcerting."

"Sure. But this is the easiest way. Since this age is closer to how you remember me. The way I was the last time we touched," Elvis said in a soft, teasing voice.

"When we watched the submarine races more than our bodies bonded, baby. It's what brought me back to you. I knew you'd help me. Besides you were already skipping about on the ethereal plane. Tuning in was easy."

"Excuse me," interrupted Posey. "Is he saying what I think he is? And if so, I thought you said you were a virgin when you got married the first time. And if I also remember correctly, you said you only went out with Elvis once."

"Twice," Kat responded.

"Then you hardly knew him."

"That's why I didn't count it. But he's right. I couldn't resist him. They say you always remember the first one."

"I can see you haven't always been completely honest with me. I certainly hope this is not a trend you plan to continue because this situation...."

Elvis laughter interrupted. "Ladies, ladies, ladies. We're a team. From now on there will be no more private conversations. I will communicate only when the three of us are tuned in. Okay Posey?"

"I'd certainly appreciate that. Some times Kat's communication system develops peculiar glitches. She doesn't let reality get in the way of remembering."

"Well, I never!" Kat sputtered.

"Hey, we're all in this together now. The first order of the day will be to purchase a small portable radio." Elvis instructed. "Then the next stop, Graceland. I'll drift on over and check the energy. Don't want any transmission or transition problems. See you girls at the house."

Static filled the car.

Chapter Nine

Long lines were already forming when Kat and Posey walked into the stark, nondescript tour building to purchase tickets.

"Except for the lighted columns, a few random plaques and an occasional picture of Elvis, this place has all the charm of a greyhound bus station," Posey observed.

"What about the colorful carpet? Greyhound doesn't have that. Exactly what did you expect anyway? This is basically a bus terminal."

"With its own souvenir shop," Posey added. "No needless running around to purchase my Elvis tee shirt and matching mug." Posey paused and looked around.

"I don't know what I expected. Something a little flashier. More Elvis."

"Well, at least we can be glad it's crowded."

"I hope crowded, confined conditions don't become a way of life."

"Stop being such a pessimist, Posey. Nothing is going to go wrong if we're careful and follow Elvis's instructions. I think the Walkman was a great idea. At least we can both hear him."

"I'm going to look like an idiot walking around with this plug in my ear," Posey complained.

"Hide the radio and pretend you're hard of hearing. If that doesn't work, tell them you're listening to Elvis tapes. Besides, have you taken a good look at this group? I don't think anything would look out of place."

Posey and Kat studied the crowd. Elvis definitely had a diverse group of followers. Most of humanity seemed to be represented.

The ticket line moved quickly. Posey and Kat were soon in the waiting area outside the ticket center. In less than thirty minutes they boarded bus forty six for the quick drive across Elvis Presley Boulevard to the mansion.

The bus entered through the open double white wrought iron gate with the musical notes and Elvis silhouettes. The entrance passed through the fieldstone wall with hundreds of names etched or sprawled with spray paint. It traveled slowly up a winding black top road lined with tall trees and stopped behind a line of identical buses unloading a short distance from the front of the mansion.

Kat and Posey had been the first to board. They were the first to depart.

"Oh goody. We'll certainly blend right in with this group," Posey said as she slowed her pace.

The walkway leading to mansion was congested with a large number of predominately Japanese tourists. The main body of the group squeezed together on the porch. The stragglers overflowed onto the front lawn of the mansion. They all had intense, strained expressions as they leaned toward a young blond woman in a tour guide uniform.

"Let's just sit here on this bench till they clear out. I've never seen anyone that walks as fast as you do," Kat said as they approached a pair of ornate, white wrought iron love seats located on each side of the walkway. A stone, Saint-Bernard-sized lion stood guard next to each bench.

"I needed to stretch my legs after the long ride over here. What did it take us? Two minutes? Besides I want to get this over with. If we don't get caught in the restricted area here, the thought of getting shot while breaking into the good doctor's sperm bank is irresistibly appealing."

"If you're so sure we're doomed to failure, why did you agree to be a part of this?"

"Temporary insanity? Or maybe just plain curiosity. Being a cat lover, you'd think I'd remember where that can lead."

Suddenly the camera-laden Japanese tourists began to move toward the now open mansion door. They disappeared quickly inside. As if on cue, the next group began to immediately form in front of the closed door. Kat and Posey waited until they were sure to be near the back.

They joined the waiting sightseers as a young man in dark blue trousers with a "Tom" name tag pinned on his light blue shirt, came through the door. He began to speak at once.

"Elvis bought Graceland in 1957 for $100,000 dollars cash."

"Not too bad for a poor boy from Mississippi," Elvis whispered in Kat's ear. She jerked her head around in the direction of the sound.

There he was, circa 1962. He hadn't aged himself more than a couple of years.

And where had she seen that outfit?

"Well Kat, I guess it's show time. Tell Posey to plug me in," Elvis instructed.

Las Vegas! Kat suddenly remembered. He'd worn that white jumpsuit in one of the shows at the Hilton International. Actually it would be a few more years, in his linear time before he'd be old enough to wear it. Kat smiled as she nudged Posey and motioned with her head toward Elvis.

"Take a squint-eyed look, just beyond my left shoulder."

Eyes narrowed, Posey peered past Kat into the instructed area.

"I can see a shadowy outline of something with sparkles bouncing off of it!" Posey exclaimed.

"Rhinestones. I thought you might be able to catch a glitter glimpse. That outfit just begs for attention. Guess you've figured out that the king's arrived."

"Radio time," Posey whispered softly. "Oh, his image is fading."

"I guess you'll just have to catch him on the air waves until you all get your vibes right."

Posey eagerly plugged in the Walkman.

"Glad you caught at least a glimmer of me, Posey. We're going to get this thing right yet. But for now, let's just hang with these folks for the first part of the tour," Elvis instructed. "We can split off when they go out in the back. After they leave Daddy's office, we'll head for the barn."

"The barn? What we're looking for is in the barn?" Posey questioned.

"It seemed appropriate since Doc Belle was a vet," Elvis answered.

Kat and Posey exchange incredulous looks before Kat blurted, "Your sperm doctor was a veterinarian!"

"Hey! We were buddies. We go back to when I bought the Circle G Ranch in '67. Actually he specialized in stud service for Tennessee Walkers, so he already had the facilities."

Their apparently disjointed conversation began to draw swift looks of disapproval from several of the nearest fans. A large redheaded woman appeared particularly interested.

Kat lowered her voice. "We're going to have to be careful about what we say. People are beginning to give us looks."

"The fact that we appear to be talking to empty space probably adds to their perplexity. I know it certainly confusing me," Posey added.

"Well, let's just try to look at each other when we talk. Even when it's to Elvis. Oh, good. We're finally going inside."

The crowd formed an irregular line as it moved forward through the open door into the entry.

Posey and Kat squeezed inside the foyer as the door was shut behind them. Tom had ascended a few steps up the white, carpeted stairway at the back of the hallway.

"Both Elvis and Lisa Marie's bedrooms are located up this stairway. It is one of several restricted areas on the premises," Tom began.

"Ask him if the barn is another one," Posey whispered.

"Hush," Kat answered as she looked around for Elvis. She immediately located him standing just inside the roped-off dining room. He turned and gave her a wistful smile as she walked toward him.

"The Christmas tree always stood in front of that window. We'd change those blue curtains to red ones," Elvis mused. "That was always my favorite time of year. We'd fill the house with poinsettias, presents and decorations, line the driveway in blue lights."

Elvis laughed softly. "Daddy said as close as we were to the airport, we'd be damn lucky if a plane didn't try to land here by mistake."

Kat opened her mouth to reply, and then noticed a young girl guide watching her. She smiled and returned to her place by Posey just as Tom was instructing everyone to turn toward the dining room.

"Did I miss anything?" she whispered.

"Well, I know how they got those two gigantic crystal chandeliers through the little bitsy doors and into the hall and dining room. If you are real nice to me, I might tell you. Was your friend with you?" Posey asked.

"He was in the dining room, but it looks like he's gone now. I hate it when I can't see him."

"Ah, I can sure sympathize with that," Posey replied indifferently. "Since Elvis is no longer interested in the dining room, why don't we skip it too?"

"I don't think we'd blend in anymore now than we did before," Kat replied looking in the direction of the hallway.

The Japanese tourists were hurriedly leaving the dining area and disappearing at the end of the corridor. A new band of sightseers came spilling through the now opened front door and began positioning themselves in front of the living room. Since the living room was directly across from the dining room, the back of the groups facing each room were almost touching.

"You and I could stand back to back facing a different room. That way no one could be sure where we really belong," Posey suggested. "Then we could rush to be first at the next stop and leave with the group in front of the Oriental Express. Sort of "The first shall be last and the last shall be first."

"That might work since they have a different guide for each room," Kat agreed. "I'll take the living room."

Kat turned around just as a petite older woman with gray hair began her canned speech.

"Elvis special ordered this fifteen foot white couch. The blue, gold and white color scheme was typical of the decor in the late sixties and early seventies."

Kat's mind drifted as she gazed at a portrait of a young Elvis that hung in a corner of the room. Then she noticed his Daddy, Vernon's portrait on the wall to the left.

Vernon Presley. What an ass!

Kat's eyes blazed as she remembered how arrogant and hateful he had been to her when she'd gone up to him in the Hilton Hotel coffee shop. She and her girlfriends had gone to Las Vegas especially to see Elvis.

I bet he never did give Elvis that message I sent with him. He just didn't want me backstage. Plain white trash in an expensive suit. All the manners and class of a share cropper. How could anything as nice as Elvis come out of him? Kat wondered, as she had so many times.

The living room guides southern drawl finally penetrated her thoughts.

"Beyond the stain glass peacocks is the intimate music room where Elvis and his friends gathered to sing their favorite songs."

Intimate? Tiny is more like it. The Memphis Mafia would have had a hard time fitting in there if they brought dates, thought Kat.

An ebony Baby Grand piano dominated the space.

"Where the hell is my white baby grand?" Elvis demanded. Startled by his sudden presence, Kat blurted "Part of the restoration."

Elvis was pensive for a moment.

"Nah, I remember now. We traded it in on this one. It really gets confusing. What was and what is," Elvis lamented.

Posey had been edging backward toward them. Her back almost touched Kat's when she turned to join them.

"If you think you're confused, try being a fan. You've been spotted at any number of fast food joints."

"I've been wondering, can you eat any of that stuff?" Kat asked.

"I just go there to sniff the smells. It's comforting."

"And nonfattening. You've definitely dropped some pounds," Posey concluded.

"Weight's not a real problem in this dimension."

"How could it be if you don't get to eat?" Kat contended.

"Right on. Soul food here has a whole new meaning. However, I still miss my fried banana and peanut butter sandwiches. Nobody seems to fix them anymore."

Elvis's reverie was interrupted as the living room/dining room guides concluded their separate information at about the same time. Each group hurried to reposition themselves at their next stop. The most aggressive of them shoved and pushed their way to the front of the line. Posey and Kat weren't quick enough to take the lead.

"We definitely missed our chance to be first. People aren't dropping off the edge of the world when they go around that corner are they?" Posey asked.

"Nah, there's a door on the left that leads to the basement," Elvis answered with a smile.

"How many more rooms until we make our great escape?" Posey questioned impatiently.

"Well, let's see. The TV and Pool Room are down there. Then I guess it's the Jungle Room and we're out," Elvis replied. "Might as well snuggle up to these people headed that way. The stairway is kind of narrow, so nobody's going anywhere in a hurry."

It was indeed a slow march to the basement door. The new guide was obviously bored as she monotoned the history of the smoked mirrored walls and ceiling leading down the stairs into the TV and pool rooms.

"If eliminating claustrophobia was really the intention, you wasted your money," Kat whispered as they descended the narrow passage. She looked up and caught her reflection. "I've certainly put mirrored ceilings to better use."

"You should see my bedroom," Elvis whispered back.

At the foot of the stairs two new guides stood at the entrance of each room. The newly arrived and the nearly departed mingled in mild confusion.

The Oriental delegation was on the right leaving the pool room.

"Well, thank God for close quarters and new opportunities. We are, of course, going to the right?" Posey speculated. She edged her way toward the pool room without waiting for conformation.

Hundreds of yards of busy colored fabric hung from the walls and draped tent-like from the ceiling. The furniture included several eras of American, European and Asian styles arranged in no particular order. However, the overwhelming feel was Arabian.

Posey looked up at the pleated ceiling. "Decorated this during your Rudolph Valentino period? Definitely a Mideastern flavor...with a pool table. Nice touch, but where are the harem girls?"

"This room is suffocating. No windows and the ceiling feels like it's about to float down on top of me," Kat gasped melodramatically.

"Well there's really not a lot to see, so I'm sure we will move on rather quickly," Posey assured her.

"I can't believe you all don't like this room. I spent some real happy times here. Watched a lot of TV in the other room. Played a lot of pool in here." Elvis sounded hurt.

"I'd enjoy it more if there weren't about thirty of us trying to crowd into it at the same time," Kat whispered.

The heavy set woman with Lucille Ball red hair pulled back in a pony tail suddenly jerked around to face them. The attentive female from the front lawn was easy to recognize. Her over- sized tee shirt proudly proclaimed, "Elvis Is Still My Main Man."

"And I'd enjoy it a whole bunch more if you all would stop whispering so loud and listen to what that young person is saying. I drove all the way up from Tupelo. This is a really special day for me." She attempted to glare at them for a moment before turning back around.

"Childhood sweetheart?" Kat muttered behind her hand. Elvis answered with a sudden slight shock to her rear.

The new guide droned on for a few more minutes. Finally, the memorized narration was over.

Next stop. The Jungle Room.

Kat and Posey were now in the front until the impatient fan from Mississippi began maneuvering past them.

"Maybe if I'm standing right by the guide I'll be able to hear over your jabbering," she announced defiantly.

"Of course that's going to eliminate the view for a few folks behind her," Kat giggled in Posey's ear as they approached the den.

Posey gave Kat a mock look of disapproval.

Finally they entered the Jungle Room. Posey smiled as she looked at the surroundings.

"Now this is the motif I had in mind for the bus station. Early savage. Chita?" Posey asked.

"What?" questioned Kat and Elvis simultaneously.

"The decorator," Posey answered.

Elvis chuckled. "I bought this in about fifteen minutes because my daddy made fun of it."

"You really should have given it more thought," Posey observed.

"I think it's kind of funky. You know, in a tasteless sort of way," Kat said defensively.

"Bad taste is not better than no taste at all," Posey replied emphatically.

Kat took a closer look around the room. It spoke for itself. Fake pagan. A Hawaiian nightmare. Artificial plants and flowers, frozen in time, mixed haphazardly with live ones. Sparse vegetation cascaded out of a stone wall with trickling water. The chairs and couch were covered in a matted gray black hide that had never been near an animal.

The furniture had hand carved arms of creatures with gapping mouths. Coordinating tables continued the theme, with a tree trunk coffee table, lacquered to a high orangish sheen, set in front of the couch. Animal knickknacks dotted the room. The walls and ceiling were carpeted.

"We use to record here. Changed colored light bulbs to fit the mood."

"Ever use a black-out light?" Posey asked." I'm sure some of this stuff would glow in the dark."

Elvis smiled.

Posey sensed it.

The new guide cleared his throat.

"The Jungle room."

Ten minutes later the group followed instructions and headed toward the back door. "This is where we split off. We won't be missed or noticed," Elvis commanded as he floated up over their heads. "I'll catch you in the yard." Then he drifted through the ceiling.

Chapter Ten

Posey and Kat tried to squeeze through the solid mass of people struggling to reach the outside. It was no use. The line moved slowly until it reached the back door. Once outside, they were immediately engulfed by the wandering masses.

"See, I told you we'd be able to mingle. Now if I can just spot Elvis," Kat said. She took in a quick overview of the big backyard of Graceland.

The atmosphere was like a small town carnival. Most appeared to be mulling around without guidance, except for a few pockets of people with a tour guide in their midst. These seemed to be clumped in three distinct areas.

"I don't suppose any of those people are checking out the barn? Posey asked as she quickly glanced around.

Elvis answered her.

"No darlin', nobody is near the barn. I'm buried over there where most of the folks seem to be praying. And the racquet ball court ought to be where those people are straight ahead of us. Maybe someday you could come back and take the tour for real, when you have more time to enjoy it," Elvis teased."

'No thanks. I'll just rent the video," Posey replied.

"Well I guess it's time to head for the barn. Just follow close behind me." His words trailed off as his image began to rapidly merge with the crowd.

"Wait a minute!" Kat shouted after him. "You're disappearing."

She narrowed her eyes and tried to focus on his ever fading figure. The mulling multitude seemed to be absorbing him. In horror, she watched Elvis vanished completely.

Posey observed Kat's shocked expression when she slowly turned to face her.

"I certainly hope that even if the visual portion of this program isn't coming in clearly, you've managed to hang on to the audio...because all I'm getting is an incredibly static filled buzzing sound."

"I guess we'll just have to find the barn by ourselves. I'm sure he'll be there."

"Sure," Posey responded." And in the meantime we have no idea where the barn is located. However, we suspect it's off limits. So of course asking directions won't call any attention to us."

"Why don't we just wander around for a while? There are only fourteen acres. How hard can it be to stumble across it?" Kat responded.

"I don't think we'll be stumbling across it unless we get off these very beaten paths," Posey replied.

The copper-topped fan from Mississippi stood about eight feet away with her hands on her hips and no-nonsense look in her eye.

"I heard you shoutin' about us disappearing. We wouldn't be out of sight if you'd pay attention and try to stay with us. I declare, one minute you're ahead of me, and then the next minute you girls are gone. Come on now. We're over by Elvis Daddy's office."

"Great!" whispered Posey. "Mother 'Really Big' Hen has found us."

"Well, at least now you won't have to rent the video. Besides, this will give Elvis a chance to notice we're not with him. He's just going to have to stop being so flighty."

Posey groaned.

An hour passed. Two guides later and no Elvis. Kat and Posey emerged from the Racquetball Building into the bright sunlight.

"I can't imagine where he is. Something must be wrong or he would have joined us by now," Kat lamented.

"He better hurry because we only have the Meditation Garden left. I'm not sure how long I can drag out my meditation," Posey concluded.

"Let's just kind of amble over in that direction..." Kat's musing was suddenly interrupted.

"Yoo-hoo! Wait a minute. I declare, I can't keep up with you girls." Red faced and out of breath, their new Mother Hen was soon by their side.

"I don't remember either of us inviting you to join us. And, no, we don't want to be part of your birthday celebration," Posey snapped.

"Well, I might just be of help to you all. Did I hear you mention looking for the barn?"

Posey and Kat exchanged disbelieving looks. How could she have overheard them? There hadn't been anyone around when they had discreetly and unsuccessfully inquired about its location.

Or had there been?

"I'm sorry. Where are my manners? My name's Early May Pruitt. I'm somethin' of an expert on Graceland. I come up here for all my birthdays and whatever special occasion I can think of. Which barn are you interested in?"

"Which barn?" They asked in unison.

"There are two of them on the property," Early May replied.

"I didn't know that," Kat managed to stammer.

"Well now, if you'll just tell me what you're looking for, maybe I can help you decide which one."

Early May eyes narrowed slightly as she faked a smile.

Kat and Posey exchanged glances of agreement. Trouble.

"Well, can I trust you to keep a secret?" Kat whispered as she leaned toward Early May. Early May responded with a slight nod of her head.

"My Daddy sold my Tennessee Walker to Elvis. You might recognize his name. Elvis called him Bear. I've always wanted to see where he spent his last days. Could you get us into the barn where he was last stabled?"

Kat's southern drawl had deepened and she sounded on the verge of tears.

"Well, you don't want that small barn in the middle of the pasture. They only keep equipment there. The horses have always been kept in the big barn over to our right. Come on. Let's walk up to the fence and I'll show you."

They walked in silence to the white fence that skirted the back acreage. Almost hidden behind a cluster of trees to the extreme right of the pasture was the barn. The stretch in between was open field.

"I assume since this is fenced off and there doesn't seem to be any people over there, that it's a restricted area." Kat appeared upset.

"I'm afraid so," Early May replied.

"We can't make it across that open space without detection," Posey observed.

"Oh, there are other ways to get there." Early May replied. "Houses on the next street back up to the stables. There's not much security back there. It's as simple as climbing over a fence."

Early May had become serious.

Kat and Posey sensed the mood shift. Without Elvis what choice did they have? Kat looked at Posey for direction, and then hesitated before stating, "I'm afraid if we leave here he'll have trouble finding us."

"We should be so lucky." Posey answered. "Just remember, the first time he found you lying in your bed in Dallas."

"Who are you girls talking about?" Early May's voice sounded strained.

"An old friend." Kat whispered.

Early May looked unconvinced. "Well, why don't we just drive on over to the next street and see what ya'll think about making a try for it?"

Chapter Eleven

Early May had insisted on driving. While she went for the car Posey and Kat agreed they would worry about getting rid of her after they found a way in. Maybe they could come back at night.

The street behind Graceland was lined with unimpressive, middle-income brick homes. Several had for sale signs in the yard. A vacant one had cardboard cut outs of Elvis in the picture window. A huge, hand-scrawled sign in the yard proclaimed "Buy here and live close to where the King lived."

"Can you imagine wanting to live next to all that confusion?" Posey asked.

"These were obviously built by the same builder, before Elvis bought the mansion," Kat observed. Newer, larger homes followed the street's curve as it headed east away from Graceland.

The only exception amid the red brick monotony was a large custom-built, two-story white brick house. A matching brick wall with black wrought iron trim encased the front yard. The view through the driveway revealed an extremely tall wooden fence that shielded the back from Graceland.

Early May stopped in front. "The barn is directly behind that house," she announced. "It's for sale and the owners are gone."

"We're going to pole vault over that fence, right?" Posey asked.

"If that's the way you want to get in. However I'd suggest ripping a few of the boards out and crawling through. Like I said, the security is fairly loose back there. You shouldn't have any trouble hiding out in the house 'til dark. The people that live here have their house listed with an old family friend. You can get the key from her. If they haven't already moved out, they're out of town most of the time anyway. By the looks of all those newspapers, I'd guess they're not home now."

"How do you know they're gone most of the time?" Posey asked suspiciously.

Early May answered quickly. "I had a girlfriend that was their personal secretary. They only wanted to pay her when they were in town and they weren't home enough for it to be a full- time job. Looks like she neglected to stop the paper before she quit."

"Well, since we're already here we might as well take a look around," Kat announced as she opened the car door. Posey reached for her arm as she slid across the seat. Early May was already scrambling out on the driver's side.

"Something tells me our new buddy has about as much regard for the truth as you sometimes do," Posey whispered to Kat.

"Yeah, I'm getting a strange feeling about her myself. Let's just play along and see where this leads."

"Probably to those confining crowded conditions that we discussed earlier."

"At least we have a new girlfriend to share it."

"That's not comforting."

The house was unoccupied. At least no one appeared as the trio inspected the backyard. The tall wooden fence extended the width of the property without a break. It was nearly new. No rotted wood to help ease the break in.

"This looks like work," Kat lamented.

"I think I noticed a short chain link fence dividing the property of the house with the Elvis paper dolls. Why don't we just go through there?" Posey suggested.

"I wonder if they still keep guard dogs chained out back?" Early May muttered to herself.

"Guard dogs? Have you actually seen them or are you just saying that to encourage us?" Posey asked.

"Oh, I've seen them all right. But it's been a long time ago." Early May answered.

"How long ago?" Kat questioned.

Early May hesitated, then took a long resigned breath and exhaled slowly.

"I use to work for a vet that treated Elvis' animals. Of course that was right before Elvis passed on," Early May nervously explained.

"I thought you were from Tupelo," Posey accused.

"I am now, but I use to live out here in Whitehaven. I guess that's why I've always felt a special bond with this place. All the times we'd come here to take care of the horses, dogs, even the chimp."

"Your vet's name wouldn't happen to be Belle, would it?" Posey inquired.

"Did you know Doc Belle?" Early May countered.

"Only by reputation," Kat answered. "How about you?"

Early May stared for a moment toward some private vision. She appeared to be struggling to control her emotions as she blinked her eyes rapidly before closing them. She cleared her throat.

"I worked for him years ago," She finally whispered.

"You seem mighty upset for a distant business associate," Posey observed.

"He hasn't been gone much more than a month," Early May snapped defensively.

"And your relationship was purely platonic?" Posey continued.

"For a while, we were very...close friends," Early May remembered sadly.

"Quite an age difference wasn't there?" Kat asked.

"You two would have made a peculiar pair of playmates. He had to have been close to eighty when he died," Posey observed.

"He was eighty two. And, yes, I guess you could say we were peculiar playmates. I went to work for him right out of high school. Just a couple of years before he retired."

"So he was kind of a father figure," Kat guessed.

Early May laughed ruefully. "Nah. He definitely was no father figure. Unless you want to consider our relationship incestuous."

Early May's revelation created the shock she had intended. For a moment, no one spoke. Kat broke the silence.

"What really brought you to Graceland today?"

"What really brought you?" Early May countered.

"I think we all need to be completely honest. Maybe we can each bring parts of the puzzle together so we can see the whole picture," Posey suggested as she gave Kat an "I have no intention of telling her everything" look.

Early May started to speak, and then changed her mind. Her eyes search the two women for a sign she could trust. She sighed heavily before finally stating, "You girls go first."

"Well, the truth is...we don't know exactly what we're looking for. Some sort of documentation confirming some secret thing Elvis did the year before he died," Kat improvised.

"We were told it's hidden somewhere in the barn at Graceland," Posey concluded.

"Who told you all that?" Early May asked as she narrowed her eyes.

"I'm afraid we can't divulge our source," Posey interjected. "Unless you have some additional information we can trade."

Early May appeared to be weighing her words. Finally she spoke. Her voice was an odd mixture of resignation and pride.

"I've got a good idea what you're lookin' for."

There was a pregnant pause before Kat blurted," Well, are you going to share?"

"It's a long story."

"We've got time."

Early May sighed, and then took a long deep breath.

"I told you Doc and I was...friendly. I use to be real pretty and about half this size. Doc and Elvis shared a thing for pretty young girls. Doc had a special reason for searching them out." She hesitated a moment before continuing. "He specialized in Tennessee Walkers stud services...had quite a sperm collection."

"From the Tennessee Walkers," Kat fished.

"Mostly," replied Early May mysteriously.

"Why don't we cut this long story down to a Reader's Digest version?" Posey suggested wearily. "At this pace we could be here 'til dark. Let's play a quick game. On the count of three we will each shout the name of any other known contributors to Doc Belle's stock pile. Okay?"

Early May and Kat nodded in agreement.

"One. Two. Three."

"Elvis!" Early May whisper loudly.

Kat and Posey observed her in silence.

"Damn you, you tricked me!" Early May glared at them in earnest.

"At least now, we all know we know," Posey replied reassuringly.

"Then you did know about it," Early May eyed them suspiciously.

"Sure. That's what we're doing here," Kat answered.

"But you don't know exactly what you're looking for?" Early May's smile was not pleasant.

"Do you know exactly what we're looking for?" Posey questioned.

Early May hesitated.

"I told you, I've got an idea," she finally admitted.

"And where did you get that idea?" Kat demanded.

"I'll exchange information with you. But this time, you go first," Early May insisted.

The calm autumn day was suddenly interrupted by a strong gust of wind that swirled into a funnel that enveloped them.

Elvis materialized during the stunned silence that followed.

"Go ahead and tell her," he instructed. "She may have some useful information."

"I hope you have a good excuse for pulling that disappearing act for so long!" Kat shouted at him.

Posey responded by quickly putting the radio plug back in her ear.

"I hope I'm interpreting your little outburst correctly. Can I have a play back of what brought it on?" Posey asked.

"I'm afraid Kat's displeased with me," Elvis answered.

"Kat's not alone. It's been a hot, unproductive, tedious day. Where have you been?"

"It's a long story."

"Shorten it."

"Okay. Tell me who you're talking to. I've seen y'all doing this off and on all morning. It's what made me start watching you," Early May demanded.

"I told you to go ahead and tell her. She'll believe you," Elvis reassured Kat.

"And why are you so sure she'll believe me?" Kat replied.

"Because of the password," Elvis answered.

"What password?" Posey and Kat inquired simultaneously.

"You're talking to Elvis, aren't you?" Early May concluded. It wasn't a question. More like an accusation. Kat decided to test her.

"Why on earth would you think that?" Kat asked.

"You said password. I know the password," Early May replied smugly.

"What is it?" Posey demanded.

"Not so fast. This time you all go first. But I promise you, if you know the magic word, I'll tell you everything I know up to this point."

Elvis laughed softly.

"Sounds fair enough to me. The password is asil eiram."

"I beg your pardon. Would you mind repeating that?" Posey said impatiently.

"Asil eiram. At least I think that's how it's pronounced."

"You have a password that you aren't sure how to pronounce? It never occurred to you that might cause a bit of a problem?" Posey asked distrustfully.

"Well, I never tried to say it aloud. I just wrote it in a letter to Doc explaining that I'd contact him when I felt it was time to defrost. Just so he'd know for sure that it was me, I gave him Lisa Marie's name backwards as a password."

"Asil eiram. It has an "open sesame" kind of sound," Kat mused.

"That's it! Oh, my lord, I can't believe this. You really are talking to him," Early May exclaimed excitedly. "Are you hearing him through that ear plug?" She asked Posey as she advanced toward her, hand outstretched.

"I want to hear."

Posey began backing away from Early May's wiggling fingers. Suddenly another burst of wind developed a whirling spout of dust between them. Startled, Early May stopped abruptly. The wind stopped with her.

"Tell her she can't hear me. That she's not tuned in properly but I'll work on it. Should be able to get it right by this evening," Elvis instructed.

"He says the reception is not quite right. He needs to align his vibrations with yours. It should be cleared up by this evening," Kat improvised.

"In the meantime, why don't we go somewhere for a quiet chat and a mint julep?" Posey suggested.

Chapter Twelve

Rockadaddy's Diner was a nostalgic return to the 50's-black and white checkered floor, blue vinyl seats with chrome accents. A large jukebox contained a menu of Elvis's records was just inside the entrance. Individual miniature jukeboxes were on the wall beside each booth. A booth opened up just as Kat, Posey and Early May walked in. Elvis materialized on the left bench next to the wall. Early May moved into him as she slid across the seat. Immediately she jerked back to the outside.

"Ooow," she exclaimed as she rubbed her left arm.

"I can sometimes make my presence felt, even when I can't be seen or heard," Elvis chuckled.

"That was him, wasn't it?" Early May whispered as she continued to rub her arm.

"I don't think that's very nice." She glared at the empty space beside her.

"She was invading my territory! But tell her I'll be gentler in the future," Elvis promised.

"Elvis is so sorry. He doesn't have complete control over his energy yet. Sometime he over amps," Kat mistranslated.

A waitress appeared before Early May could reply. Instead, she turned her attention to the menu.

"I'm a might hungry. Think I'll just order a little something to tide me over."

A double cheeseburger, large fries and a chocolate milkshake later, she was ready to talk. She pushed aside the dirty dishes then paused dramatically before starting her story.

"I went to work for Doc in 1975. Right out of high school. I'd moved up here from Tupelo and was living with my Mama's sister. Doc was already in his early sixties. My Aunt Beth and my parents all figured he was passed the age of tempting or temptation. Boy were they big time wrong."

"That's another thing we had in common. Doc and I both had a burning love for pretty, young things," Elvis added wistfully.

"I'm sure under different circumstances I'd find your romantic history fascinating. However we are a little pressed for time," Posey said, addressing Early May and Elvis simultaneously.

Annoyed at being interrupted, Early May smirked, and then asked defiantly, "You know about Doc Belle's partner?"

"Sort of," Kat hedged.

"How can you sort of know something like that? You either do or you don't."

"Tell her I hadn't filled in all the blanks," Elvis instructed.

"Elvis has been selectively feeding us information. Why don't you tell us what you know about Doc's partner?"

Early May rubbed her left arm while she silently studied them.

"Oh hell! Why not? I haven't been getting anywhere but confused on my own."

Early May paused again, before launching into her story. "Twenty five plus years ago, Doc brought a young vet into his practice. Todd Ledbetter was just out of Texas A & M. Later, Doc sold him the practice...but not the stud farm. However, it was stipulated that he would get the farm at Doc's death. You do know that's where Elvis'... popsicles are."

"That's what we assumed," answered Posey.

"Were you working for Doc when young Doctor Todd came into the practice?" Kat asked.

"Yeah. I guess that's why he contacted me. Doc left him the farm but with some of the records missing. When Doc found out he was dying he'd shipped them to me. Doc had confided in me about Elvis' liquid legacy almost from the beginning. As a matter of fact, I was the first potential mama. But Elvis never bothered to contact Doc...ask him why."

"I tried, but the only time his guard was down enough for me to get through to him he'd had a few drinks. My showing up always unnerved him so that he'd end up drunk. The next morning he couldn't tell whether I'd made contact or if he'd been hallucinating."

"Elvis says he did try, but Doc developed a drinking problem and the next morning was unsure about his visits," Kat explained.

"He definitely developed a drinking problem. And he did ramble on about dreaming about Elvis all the time. It got to be pretty pathetic."

"Let's get back to those records Doc sent you," Posey urged. "Just the ones that pertain to Elvis."

"Well, actually, all of the ones he sent me pertained to Elvis, one way or another. There was the letter with the password in it. And a strange journal with some kind of code system. I've got it with me. I've figured out some of it. Maybe we can figure out the rest together."

Early May began to dig into her oversized purse. Finally, she pulled out a gray and red ledger book, flipped through the pages, and then handed the open book to Kat.

"See the lines I've highlighted in yellow? The doc/Gralnd/bn I interpreted to mean document at Graceland. Couldn't quite figure out bn, but since running into you all I'm pretty sure it stands for barn. That other gibberish probably gives the exact location. It makes no sense to me."

"lrg/rk/nr/br/stl," Kat read out loud.

"Large rock near Bear's stall," Elvis interpreted.

"Large rock near Bear's stall?" Posey repeated. "Exactly what's under the rock?"

"Doc and I figured that my sperm looked like everybody else's. If we didn't document that it was mine for sure, we'd have a hard time peddling our story. We decided to keep the proof separate from the pudding, so to speak."

"What did he say?" Early May asked impatiently.

"It's just as you thought. It's identity documentation," Kat answered.

"What kind?" Early May insisted.

"It's a notarized letter in my hand writing. Actually, Early May's the one that notarized it," Elvis replied.

"He says you notarized his hand written letter."

"I'd think that would be something you'd remember. Are you a notary?" Posey inquired suspiciously.

"I was. Doc insisted I become one. But I never paid much attention to the stuff he had me stamp. I just put my seal where he told me to. Now that you mention it, there was one letter that caught my eye. I remember catching a sentence or two off a handwritten "to whom it may concern" note that Doc rushed passed me. I notice it because of the signature. Elvis Aron Presley. I even asked Doc about it. He was real jumpy. Told me to stamp it and forget it." Early May paused, and then continued. "That explains why he included my notary log in the packet with the records he sent me."

"How much does Doctor Todd know about all this?" Kat asked.

"I'm not sure. He contacted me about the special King Kong vials in the freezer and the missing records. I played dumb."

"That must have been a stretch for you," Posey quipped.

"Don't get nasty with me," Early May warned. "Or I won't be useful." She folded her arms and scowled at Posey.

"Posey, for heaven's sake, keep your dubious wit in check. Please go on Early May."

Obviously irritated, Early May continued. "I started getting real curious, so I decided to come on up here and do some checking around. It seems Dr. Todd Ledbetter has an expensive dog and pony show going on. He has lost, big time, at the dog tracks in West Memphis and the horse track in Hot Springs. Owes some real bad guys a bundle."

"You think he suspects the true content of the vials?" Kat asked.

"It wouldn't surprise me. Doc could get pretty loose lipped when he'd had too much to drink. Toward the end, seemed like he was plastered every time I came up to visit. Besides, Elvis was the reason Todd persuaded his parents to buy into the business in the first place. Anything to do with Elvis intrigued him. He was a huge fan. I don't think he ever forgave Doc for Elvis's early departure. Blamed him for it, somehow. That's one reason Doc took early retirement. He and Todd fought all the time."

"Where do you think Doc kept the Elvis file?" Posey asked. "Could Todd have run across it?"

"If he went looking for it, it probably would have been easy enough to find. Doc kept most of his private records in the office at the farm. Todd had a key because they operated the stud service from there. And the files weren't in the package Doc sent me."

"Todd has known about my frosty delight, almost from the beginning. That's why his parents paid so much for the partnership. 'Course they had a truck load of money. Gave him just about anything he wanted. In the beginning, he was torn between selling it to the highest bidder and waiting to impregnate a future wife. Gambling debts didn't figure into his plans. He developed that little problem later," Elvis interjected.

"They were really labeled King Kong vials?" Kat questioned incredulously.

"That was Doc's idea. I told you he had a drinking problem," Early May answered.

"King Kong, for the King," Elvis explained. Kat and Posey looked at each other then began to shake their heads in amusement.

"What else is Elvis telling you?" Early May demanded.

"He said that Todd has known about them almost from the beginning," Posey answered.

"How does he know that?" asked Early May.

"Good question. Would you care to answer, your majesty?" Posey asked.

"When I got to the barn this mornin', there were a couple of beefy lookin' boxer types crashing around, tearing into stuff. I decided to hang and see what was coming down. Every now and then I'd give them a little prod. You could say my behavior was shocking" Elvis teased.

Posey looked at Kat and rolled her eyes.

"What did he say?" Early May pressured.

"He's just explained to us how electrifying he can be. Apparently you aren't the only one he's used that little shock treatment on," Posey explained.

"Anyway, it all led back to a rendezvous with Dr. Ledbetter. What I overheard made me curious, so I skipped into the other dimension and found Doc Belle. That poor guy is really confused. His idea of the hereafter seems to be to stay drunk all the time. However, he did remember some conversations he and Todd had that helped me arrive at my own conclusions...

Incidentally that's the reason I was gone so long. Hope you girls will forgive me."

Kat reached across the table to pat his hand reassuringly. Her hand glided through his energy field and tapped the table instead.

"Can't you thicken up a little bit?" She asked as she drew her hand back.

"Well if I could darlin, I wouldn't start with my hand."

"Come to think of it, that wouldn't be my first choice either," Kat teased back.

"Stop that talkin' without tellin'. You all are going to have to keep me better informed than this," Early May demanded

"Trust me; you have not missed a thing," Posey assured her.

"You let me be the judge of that!" Early May snapped.

"We do have some potentially pressing problems that we need to think about," Elvis said thoughtfully. "Those two guys in the barn this morning will be back. That letter of verification is real important to Dr. Ledbetter. The vials aren't collateral without it."

"How did those two fellows get in there anyway?" Kat asked.

"They took some slats out of a fence that backs up to the property," Elvis answered.

"Not the same place we were earlier? I didn't see any loose boards," Posey said.

"They nailed everything back as they left. It should be easier for you all to pry them open the second time," Elvis answered.

"What do you think we should do next?" Kat asked.

"Go back to that house. No doubt they'll use that way again. We need to get ready for them."

"Why don't we just go through that way now? Get the letter and destroy it?" Posey suggested.

"Well darlin', I hate to tell you this. They've done some remodeling at Graceland. The stone's gone and they've poured a concrete floor where it used to be," Elvis replied reluctantly.

"Great. How do we know that the letter hasn't already been found?" Posey asked.

"Because I could see the metal box was still a couple of feet down where I'd buried it."

"When had you planned to tell us that we were going to need more equipment than our bare hands?" Posey asked.

"Or were you going to let us find out for ourselves?" Kat complained.

"What are you all talking about? What kind of equipment are we going to need? For what?" Early May interrupted.

"Oh, just a little something to break through a concrete floor. You didn't happen to pack a jackhammer for your trip up here, did you?" Posey asked sardonically.

"I thought what we were looking for was in the barn. The only place concreted in there is where they keep the saddles and such."

"Not any more," Posey retorted.

"Apparently they've done some remodeling," Kat added.

"Oh, shit! Now what?" Early May exclaimed.

"Well girls, if you'll just be patient, I'll explain my plan," Elvis interjected.

"Elvis has a plan," Kat repeated to Early May.

Chapter Thirteen

"Have you found that address yet?" Early May asked as they drove slowly down Elvis Presley Blvd. "I can't believe you just stole the book out of that phone booth."

Kat was seated on the passenger side flipping through the yellow pages.

"I can't believe there was one to steal. If you'd remembered the last name of the little old lady who has the house listed, we'd already be there. We're lucky her first name is unusual."

"You should count your blessings that I'm here to help. You wouldn't be this far along," Early May countered belligerently.

Posey leaned forward from the back seat. "Excuse me, Ms. Pruitt; do I need to remind you who is in communication with the King?"

Early May twisted her head toward the back. She and Posey exchange brief hostile glances.

"Truce time! We got a job to do," Kat ordered. "I just hope our real estate lady is a little financially stressed. If she needs the commission it will be easier to deal with her. After we find out where her office is, Elvis can check her out."

"Just remember our time is limited. I need to be hanging over at the barn in case that pair of bears shows up sooner than we thought they would," Elvis interjected.

"Here! I've got it!" Kat shouted. "Maple Melton Real Estate. She's just up the street a couple of blocks. We'll keep driving toward it while you take a surveillance flight."

"This is the way I like to do business. In a flash!" Elvis laughed, and then disappeared.

Later that afternoon, Elvis was standing with his arms folded, leaning toward the door when the maroon Lincoln pulled into the strip shopping center. He popped into the back seat as the car rolled to a stop.

"You girls look real nice. Did you dress up for Miss Maple? She's a bit slow but I expect she'll be here anytime now.

"I want you to know it was damned hard trying to find something to wear that I could discreetly hide this walkman," Posey groused.

"I was worried when we first found the office closed, but now I'm glad Miss Maple had her phone transferred to her house. That gave us time to change cars and clothes. Now we look more like we've got a little Texas money to spend," Kat said, as she turned toward Elvis in the back seat. "Early May's going to give us time to pick up the key. Then she's going to park across the street from the house. We're going to have to find a way to get the key from Miss Maple, long enough to have a duplicate made. I just hope she is as far out of the loop as you say she is."

"She's a sweet old thing that should have retired a few years back. I'm going to have to think of something nice to do for her when this is all over. Bless her heart; she's blind as a bat. Just hope she doesn't have a problem driving over here. The state wouldn't renew her driver's license but they couldn't take away her car."

"How do you know that?" Kat asked.

"She talks to herself."

"Not to change the subject. I suppose the surveillance flight over the barn didn't pick up any enemy activity?" Posey guessed.

"Nah, nothing going on except the horses eatin' and excretin'," Elvis answered with a chuckle.

A yellow cab pulled into the shopping center and stopped behind the Lincoln. The driver jumped out and opened the door for a diminutive, elderly woman dressed in an outmoded, expensive, lightweight, purple suit with a bright orange blouse. Atop her lavender-colored hair was a red pillbox hat.

"Poor baby. Must be color blind too," Elvis said sadly.

"She needs a different hair dresser or a different rinse," Posey observed.

Maple Melton walked passed the car to the door of her office where she began to fumble with her keys. She unsuccessfully tried each key attached to the oversized key ring. The process appeared to be happening in slow motion.

"I can't handle this any more," Kat said impatiently, as she bounded out of the car. She stuck her head back in. "I've seen my future and it's pretty scary." She hurriedly turned and walked toward the entrance to the real estate office.

"Hi, I'm Kat McBride. Are you Miss Melton?" Kat extended her hand.

Maple Melton placed her small, frail hand into Kat's out stretched one. Her clouded blue eyes looked enormous behind her magnified glasses.

"I seem to have an overabundance of keys. I really should have discarded half of these a long time ago. Yes, I'm Maple Melton. Please, just call me Maple. I declare, child, I can't tell you how glad I am you said you wanted to drive. I'm having a little car trouble."

Kat was surprised by the overwhelming nostalgia that flooded her senses. It was as if she were greeting a once, close friend. One who had grown old since they had last been together.

"Do you need to get into your office for the keys to the house or do you have them with you?"

"Oh, no, I don't need anything from in there. Buddy and Ruth moved out last weekend. They left me their set of keys. I have them separate, on their own key ring."

"That's great! My friend is waiting for us in the car." Kat placed a protective hand under Miss Melton's arm and turned her in that direction.

Miss Melton continued, "I don't have one of those fancy electronic cards you need to get into the lockboxes with now days. I had a hard enough time when it was just dialing certain letters of the alphabet to open the box. Anyway, if an agent wants to show the house they have to come by my office to pick up a key. To my notion, that's a safer way to do business."

"You can certainly keep track of the showings better that way," Kat agreed, as they approach the passenger side of the waiting vehicle.

"Posey, why don't you let Miss Melton sit in the front beside me?"

"Good idea!" Posey started to gather her things for the move to the back.

"Why I'd just as soon sit in the back with that nice young man," Miss Melton said as she lowered her glasses to the end of her nose and peered past the brim into the back seat.

Kat and Posey were wonder struck. She could see Elvis?

"I'd be honored ma'am," Elvis replied sliding over to his extreme left.

Maple Melton situated her body and belongings in the rear seat. She took her thick glasses off and held them in her lap as she scrutinized the young man smiling at her from across the way.

"You look a lot like Elvis. Funny, I can see you clearer without my glasses. Is that who you are? Or are you one of those impersonators."

"Oh, I'm the real thing Miss Maple," Elvis replied tenderly.

"It's almost my time isn't it? That why I can see you so clearly." There was no trace of sadness in her voice.

"I'm afraid so."

"Oh, don't be afraid, son. My body and my money have just about run out at the same time my spirit's leaving. I always wanted to break even in the end. Looks like I got my wish."

Amazed at Miss Maple's unruffled ability to see Elvis plus her nonchalant attitude toward death, Kat and Posey gave the back seat conversation their rapt attention. They were teary eyed when Miss Maple looked up at them.

"Don't go crying for me. One of these days you'll find out what blessed relief surrender is. Now tell me, what we are really doing, because we sure as the devil aren't house hunting."

There would be no need for a duplicate key. Maple Melton could be trusted.

Chapter Fourteen

"Glory be and praise our angels, there's some furniture here! I really wasn't looking forward to lounging around on the floor. Bless Buddy's heart for not taking it all," Miss Maple declared.

"Why do you suppose they didn't?" Posey asked.

"They probably bought a smaller place and didn't have room for everything. Sellers usually get rid of what's left when they get a contract on the house," Kat answered.

Elvis floated down the stairs toward them. "There's a whole bedroom upstairs furnished. And a few odds and ends in the others."

"That's wonderful!" exclaimed Miss Maple. "Now we can take turns resting. If any one gets tired, that is."

"It'll soon start to get dark. Early May ought to show up any time now," Kat said.

"I'm going to make a quick reassurance flight over the barn. I'll be back before you miss me," Elvis announced.

"Before you fly away son, you might want to consider a wardrobe change. Something black to go with the coming night... Oh I know! That wonderful black leather outfit that you wore on one of your TV specials," Miss Maple suggested.

"That's a good idea. I'm getting a little tired of this white jumpsuit," Elvis agreed.

"How's this?" His white jumpsuit changed into black leather as he asked the question.

"Oh mercy! That attire makes me wish I were your interesting older woman. Of course, we would have to go back nearly a half-century. I don't imagine that shifting energy is a problem where you are?"

"No ma'am. We have more of a problem keeping it all pulled together after we alter the force field."

"What a delightful prospect!" Miss Maple exclaimed.

"I beg your pardon?" Elvis looked puzzled.

"After my...crossing, I won't ever have to bother with zippers or buttons again," Miss Maple explained.

"Early May just pulled up," Posey informed them from her lookout by the picture window next to the living room drapes.

"Do we want her to leave or stay?"

"Leave. But let's keep it as simple as possible. Just tell her Miss Maple is an ally and the key is not a problem. If anything comes down, we'll contact her," Elvis instructed. "Now ladies, I really must go take an overview of the barn. I'll be back in a heart beat," His image faded instantly.

A brief moment of silence passed.

"Elvis has definitely left the building," Miss Maple sighed. She and Kat exchanged smiles.

Chapter Fifteen

The grandfather clock in the hall signaled the hour. Kat silently counted each of the ten strokes.

"Do you think those goons are waiting for the neighborhood to go to sleep?" Kat asked no one in particular.

"That's what I figure," Elvis answered, "There hasn't been a sign of them at the stable."

"If there is a concrete floor covering the area where the proof is hidden and the marking stone is gone, how are they going to know where to search?" Posey asked.

"Doc told Todd that the documentation was hidden by Bear's stall. They pretty much trashed the above ground area this afternoon. And I've been planting hints about hidden treasure in Todd's mind all afternoon. It won't be much of a reach for him to decide to go underground. Once they dig it up, we'll just take it away from them. Beats trying to shovel it out of there ourselves."

"Can't you do something to kind of levitate it up to us?" Kat wondered.

"It's not quite that simple. However, I am getting more of a handle on how to keep this energy focused into form. Can you make me out yet, Posey?"

"I've noticed if you are in front of a light background I can see a shadowy something. But dark on dark...nothing."

Posey's eyes were squinted as she peered into the section that Kat appeared to be addressing.

"Well children, if you all will excuse me, I'm going to retire to the upstairs bedroom. If the vigil picks up, someone come and alert me," Miss Maple announced wearily as she started ascending the stairs.

"Sure thing, Miss Maple. I won't let you miss any of the action," Elvis answered.

"Such a sweet boy," Miss Maple said to herself as she continued the climb to the second floor.

Chapter Sixteen

Dawn spread like a lumpy gray blanket that hovered over most of Shelby County. Heavy moisture hung in the air, a sure sign of the coming rain.

Miss Maple slowly descended the stairs. Midway down, she paused to observe the sleeping pair below her. Posey lay stretched back in the large leather recliner. Kat was in the fetal position on the matching couch. Elvis was nowhere in sight.

Maybe I should return to the bedroom and wait until I hear them stirring, Miss Maple thought.

Suddenly Kat set upright on the couch. She quickly glanced around the room, and then noticed Miss Maple on the stairway.

"Do you know where Elvis is?"

"I'm sorry my dear, but I haven't a clue," whispered Miss Maple. "I don't suppose you'd let me sleep through anything?"

"Just a lot of false alarms. The last thing I remember was Elvis heading back to the barn. I'm not sure what time it was, but it was jet black outside."

Posey stirred in the chair then struggled sleepily to an upright position. "Tell me I've had a nightmare and we're really still in Dallas."

"'Fraid not," Kat answered.

"Why do you suppose they didn't show last night?" Miss Maple asked.

"Elvis thinks they might not have had access to the right kind of equipment to break through the concrete floor. Or, even if they have the equipment, they decided the noise would bring security in a hurry."

"Or, they may not have picked up on the buried treasure theory yet. So, what is our next move?" Posey asked.

"I would imagine we need to wait for Elvis's return. He's probably gathering information," Miss Maple suggested.

"We also need to get out of here before the work day starts. I can just see the look on an agent's face when she brings clients through the door and we're here to greet them in our slept-in clothes and uncombed hair. I doubt we could come up with a very convincing story."

"Oh, you don't have to worry about that, dear. I don't have it on lockbox and I have the only keys, remember?" Miss Maple answered.

"You're sure there aren't any extras floating around with agents that forgot to bring them back?" Kat worried.

"Oh heavens, now that you mention it, there was a young agent that came by the house a few days ago. I'm not sure she did return the extra set."

The sound of the doorbell made a jarring intrusion into the conversation. They exchanged glances in the brief silence that followed.

"Oh pooh," Miss Maple scoffed. "There's not an agent in town that would be showing at this hour. It's not even broad daylight."

"A neighbor could have turned us into the police for trespassing," Posey suggested half-heartedly.

"There's only one way to know for certain. Here goes," Kat muttered while she walked toward the door. She barely unlocked it when an unkempt, upset Early May barged in. Her curly red hair fanned out in all directions.

"Can I assume, since I didn't hear from you all, that not a damned thing happened last night?"

"Nice hairdo," Posey called from the den.

"Don't start with me this morning. I broke my only elastic band. After spending the night in you all's motel room and laying around in these clothes, I'm not in the mood for any smart-ass mouthing."

"If you'll take a good look, you'll see that none of us have changed clothes. And we can all match your mood," Kat replied. "Posey told you we'd call if there was any activity. By the way, this is Miss Maple Melton. Early May Pruitt, Miss Maple."

Early May ignored the introduction. "I couldn't sleep a wink. Just tossed and tumbled all night."

"Your clothes certainly validate that," Posey observed.

Early May shot Posey a "watch it" look.

"We all need to freshen up a bit," suggested Miss Maple. "Why don't you drop me off at my place, go clean up, and change your attire. When you return to my house, we can have coffee and discuss our next move."

"I didn't come prepared to spend the night. I don't have a change," Early May complained.

"We'll all chip in and buy you a new tee shirt," Posey suggested sarcastically.

"Shouldn't we wait until Elvis comes back?" Kat asked.

"I've been thinking about that. He is probably tuned into our frequency enough by now to pick us up anywhere. I presume it's rather like one of those bug things police put on cars they want to follow," contemplated Miss Maple.

Elvis's laughter preceded him.

"You're right on about the harmonized frequency. Kind of an ethereal eavesdropping." Elvis had not changed out of the previous night's apparel either. He appeared in black leather on the stairs near Miss Maple.

"Where have you been?" Kat demanded.

"I decided to pay Dr. Ledbetter a nocturnal visit. I think my daytime hints about the hidden treasure were a shade too subtle, so I invaded his dreams."

"Good heavens! You can do that at will?" inquired Posey.

"Pretty much. It's actually a lot easier than daylight manifestations. Sort of like lucid dreaming is for you," Elvis explained. "You know, the dreams you know you're dreaming and can control the action."

"Not that anybody cares, but I can hear him," Early May whispered in awe.

"Can you see me, Early May?" Elvis asked.

"I can see something dark and hazy next to Miss Maple," Early May replied. She continued to peer in that direction.

"And what about you, Posey?" Elvis asked.

"It's weird, but I didn't even notice that I didn't have my walkman plugged in. Yeah, I can hear you but your image looks almost like a photograph's negative. I guess it will develop into something more visible later on. Right?" Posey concluded.

"That's what I'm working on," Elvis answered.

"Okay, tell me about the dream you gave the good doctor," Kat insisted impatiently.

"I was very direct. Didn't give him any veiled symbols. Basically I just told him where to dig...then instructed him to recall the dream vividly."

"So you can dance around in my dreams anytime you want?" Kat asked wistfully.

"Only if there is a real purpose involved and if it's for the highest and best good of all concerned. It's not a play time activity," Elvis answered.

"Who determines the highest and best good?" interrupted Miss Maple.

"Once you arrive here, you're gifted with complete inner knowing. But you still have choices. That's one of the things that decide if you stay earthbound or travel to the next dimension."

"You must have made some incredibly bad choices after you arrived there. You're still around after twenty plus years," added Posey.

"Bad choices aren't the only reason you hang around," Elvis answered gently. "If you can help undo some damage you've done or if you can just be of service to someone, watch over someone, you may decide you want to stay. There's a whole bevy of guardian angels that have decided to hover here. Then there are scattered groups of people that died violently. Most of them think they are in a nightmare and will wake up eventually. Some others have remained here to earn extra credit, so they can get a passing grade, so to speak. Hanging here is not an easy way to pay a karmic debt. It's better if you can work it out during your earth time."

"Speaking of time, do you think we'll have enough to freshen up before any activity starts?" Miss Maple asked.

"I'm sure I can slow them down if they show up before you return. I doubt they'll be back until dark. No sense in you all staying around here all day. I'll keep you posted," Elvis answered with a smile.

"How do you suppose they'll mask the noise once they start jack hammering?" Posey wondered.

"Hopefully we'll find out this evening," Elvis answered.

"Why don't you ladies drop me off, then go change into something more comfortable? It shouldn't take us long to tidy up. I can fix us a nice brunch." Miss Maple began to dig in her purse. "Here Early May, take this twenty and buy yourself a new top. I'm sure a clean tee shirt will make you feel better. When you find one, you can come back to my place."

Early May took the money without hesitation. "Thanks Miss Maple. I didn't plan on staying up here this long, so I am running low on cash."

Chapter Seventeen

Miss Maple stood by her kitchen window watching the heavy dark clouds drift on the pale gray sky as the light dimmed toward evening.

"This is so peculiar. The forecast for today was decreasing clouds with little chance of rain. A cool front was on the way. It's been so hot and muggy I was really looking forward to a change in temperature. I declare, sometimes I think the weathermen just throw a bunch of forecasts into a huge hat and draw one a day."

"Why don't we turn on the Weather Channel? Maybe they have a local update," Posey suggested as she walked toward the television on the counter.

Across the bottom of the forming picture was a moving ribbon announcing the gathering storm.

Posey read the forecast out loud. "Warning: radar indicates heavy rain and thundershowers. Tornado watches for Shelby County in effect until 8:00 p.m."

"This is a strange time of year to be having these kinds of storm systems. It is usually a spring and summer occurrence. By September, we're normally past all this. Perhaps we should return to our lookout before the full force of the storm hits," Miss Maple suggested.

A sudden loud roll of thunder rumbled ominously through the house. An enormous lightning bolt punctuated the fading sound, illuminating the kitchen.

Elvis appeared.

"I agree with Miss Maple. Now would be a real good time to return to the watching place."

"You didn't have anything to do with our strange weather, did you dear boy?" Miss Maple asked affectionately.

"Not in a serious way. Since our work crew seemed to be having a hard time figuring how to muffle the sound, I decided to sow a few water seeds in some clouds. Thought a little rain and thunder might cover some of the noise. Of course, I don't have any control over the weather once it's started. Hope this one doesn't get out of hand."

"Are you in any danger, flitting about in this kind of storm?" Kat asked.

"No permanent damage. But a lightning strike could dissipate my energy field. It might interfere with reception."

"That's a happy thought. What if it happens during one of our needier moments?" Posey asked.

"Well girls, to tell you the truth, I've never been hit by lightning, so I'm not exactly sure what kind of sparks will fly. Let's just hope Mother Nature doesn't get too carried away with her air show."

"I hope the rain doesn't discourage them. I need to get back to Tupelo," Early May fretted.

"They've already rented the equipment. I'd bet money they'll show tonight. Rain or moonshine," Elvis added.

"Did you overhear any specific plans?" Kat asked.

"They're bringing a guy named Hercules with them. I'm guessing that's a nickname since he's going to carry the jackhammer and help dig up the box. Must be a pretty big boy," Elvis replied.

"So the dream work accomplished what you needed." Posey concluded.

Elvis chuckled. "It got them headed in the right direction. They still might need a little sting to steer them to the exact location."

"And you're the guy with the juice," Posey added.

Elvis laughed, then noticed his picture peering out from Early May's new top.

"Nice tee shirt, Early May. I like the sentiment."

"It's a night shirt. They didn't have a tee shirt in my size." She looked down at the yellow top. A young Elvis appeared in the middle of a huge heart. Above it was written, "Elvis is king of my heart." Another large heart with a winking Elvis was located on the back. "I'll see you in your wildest dreams" was written under it.

"We're wasting dry weather. Let's get our stuff together and go before the down pour starts," Kat suggested.

"Why don't we take something to nibble on in case we get hungry?" Early May asked.

"When are you not hungry?" Posey answered.

"I've already started a basket. Just give me a minute to get the cold items out of the refrigerator," Miss Maple intervened. "I've prepared some peanut butter and banana sandwiches. We can fry them later. Elvis will at least enjoy the aroma while they're cooking."

"That's mighty thoughtful of you. It's been awhile," said Elvis.

"Please tell me that's not our only choice." Posey pleaded.

"Of course not, dear. That's just a little treat for the boy."

Chapter Eighteen

The schizophrenic wind blew the pelting rain in all directions. Marble size hail added weight and noise to the mixture. Thunder exploded lightning bolts that illuminated the darkened early evening sky.

The untouched food basket set on the kitchen counter. Even Early May was uninterested in its contents.

Elvis had been gone for more that an hour. Each minute seemed to feed the storm's appetite for destruction. Tree branches blew past the windows in a bizarre twisting dance. The house itself trembled with each malicious attack.

Posey broke the uncomfortable silence.

"No one in his right mind is going to be out in this weather. I wish we could just phone Elvis to come on back. What could he be doing all this time at the barn?"

"Assuming he made it to the barn," Kat added pessimistically.

"This weather is unsettling. I hope he didn't encounter a lighting strike. It might take some time to regroup his energy," Miss Maple interjected.

"We can be thankful no one has shown up while he's gone," Early May concluded, as she walked to the back window.

"Uh oh. I spoke too soon."

Immediately Early May was joined by the others. They watched silently as an unmarked white van backed into the driveway. A trio of large men scrambled from its interior. The largest man hurried to the back of the van and opened the door. He handed out two shovels then casually swung a jackhammer over his shoulder and followed his companions through the rain, toward the back fence.

"It's not hard to tell which one is Hercules. However, his buddies aren't exactly shrimps," Posey observed.

"I just wish we knew for sure where Elvis is. I can't imagine trying to take anything away from those three," Kat fretted.

"Seduction is not a choice, unless you remembered to pack your black leather outfit with the whip and chain accessories," Posey quipped.

"This is no time for your questionable wit," Kat scoffed.

"Maybe if we held hands in a circle and concentrated on sending Elvis a message to contact us, we might get through to him," Miss Maple suggested.

"Anything beats standing around here doing nothing," Early May answered. She took Miss Maple's outstretched hand and offered her other hand to Kat.

"Okay, let's think of a single sentence for all of us to concentrate on," Kat instructed, as she took Early May's hand and reached for Posey's reluctant one.

"Why not a single word. Help!" Posey offered.

"We could start with help. Maybe add, come back now," Miss Maple concurred.

"That certainly says it all," Early May agreed.

They held hands as they formed a circle. The wind ceased as if to honor their intention. Uneasy calm surrounded the house. The rain became a mist. Time became immobile, stuck in the present moment.

Elvis did not appear.

"Perhaps if we chanted the words. The vibration might reach him," Kat suggested.

"Why don't we just sing and dance "Ring Around The Roses" and be done with it?" Posey grumbled.

"Have you noticed how still it has gotten?" Miss Maple whispered.

"I have," Early May answered solemnly. "I just hope we don't hear a sound like train rumbling, because the closest thing they have to a storm cellar is the basement." She walked to the back window to check the sky. Her eyes searched for what she did not want to see. A funnel cloud. Nothing but a plaster of gray punctuated with enormous, threatening black clouds. An opening in the fence where slats had been removed brought her attention back to the present purpose.

"Looks like they've made it through the fence."

"Things sure quieted down at a bad time for them," Posey observed.

"And subsequently for us," Kat added.

"I fear this may be just a temporary lull," Miss Maple's voice trembled.

"You sound a little alarmed. I thought you were looking forward to death. Or did I misinterpret something?" Posey asked.

"My dear, it's not death I fear. I just have no desire to reenact Dorothy's trip to Oz."

Early May walked to the built-in big screen television next to the fireplace and switched it on.

"Surely there will be an update on the weather. At least we'll know what's happening around us. It may be time to go down into the basement."

As if on command, the voice preceded the forming picture. "We interrupt this broadcast to bring you a special weather bulletin. Multiple funnel clouds have been sighted south of Memphis. A twister was observed near highway 78 north of Olive Branch, Mississippi. Another was sighted near Hernando, Mississippi, on Highway 55. None have touched down. However, a tornado warning is in effect for Shelby County. Stay tuned for weather updates."

"How close are those towns from here?" Posey asked.

"We could walk," Early May spoke in a hushed tone.

"It's hard to tell where they stop and Memphis begins," added Kat.

"The only thing between Memphis and Olive Branch is Whitehaven. Unfortunately, we appear to be in the storms path," Miss Maple commented uneasily.

"Ladies, you called?" Elvis asked as his image appeared on the big screen.

"Where have you been?" Kat implored.

"Why darlin', I've been hangin' at the barn."

"You've been gone so long; we've all been concerned. Especially since the weather has turned so dreadful." added Miss Maple.

"To tell you the truth, that's the reason I hadn't tried to make it back. Can't seem to keep it all together in high winds."

"That the reason you've chosen this medium to contact us?" Miss Maple guessed.

"Exactly. Besides the diggers have shown up. They need my attention if we're ever going to get to the bottom of this."

"We're under a tornado warning," Posey emphatically interjected.

"What's the matter Posey? Are you afraid you might be joining me prematurely?"

"Do you know something I don't?" Posey commanded.

Elvis laughed. "I'm not a fortune teller. The future isn't any clearer from this perspective than it is from yours. Learn to tune in to your higher power and go with your knowing."

"Well my knowing tells me that we are in the path of an on coming tornado and we should get the hell out of Dodge. Excuse me, Memphis," Posey shot back.

"You can't out run it. Your best bet is to get in the basement and wait it out. Take your radio with you so you'll know what's going on," Elvis advised.

"What about you? If you can't handle high winds, a tornado will be a real bitch," Kat said apprehensively.

"I've got a job to do. When the box is up, I'll just become part of the atmosphere and ride the winds till they calm down." Elvis chuckled. "The roller coaster was my favorite ride at the Fairgrounds. Bet this beats that for thrills."

"With you not around, what exactly are we suppose to do about getting the information away from those three thugs?" Posey questioned.

"Maybe the storm will just skirt us and we won't have to worry about that," Elvis answered calmly. "Regardless, I'll keep in touch."

His image faded from view as a distant reverberation grew closer. Strong gale driven vibrations rumbled toward them. The preview of high winds performed a sadistic dance with tree limbs and debris. Mother Nature was in a nasty unpredictable mood.

"To the basement immediately!" Miss Maple shouted.

"I'll get the basket," Early May announced. Posey and Kat quickly followed Miss Maple toward the basement door. Early May was right behind them as they descended the stairs.

Chapter Nineteen

The four women huddled together listening to the cacophony of disruptive sounds above them. The walkman, tuned to the highest volume, sputtered bits of information and an occasional whole sentence before static filled the airwaves.

"...confirmed reports of a tornado touch down near Graceland...the mansion remains intact. However a barn..." The voice faded as static covered the remaining announcement.

"That's a great time for the message to disintegrate. Not only is it on top of us, but Elvis may be getting the ride of his afterlife," Posey grumbled.

"I hope he's not being pushed to a dimension he can't return from," Kat added.

"Do you suppose the box had been elevated before the tornado hit? If so, perhaps the letter was destroyed," Miss Maple wished aloud.

"If that scenario is feasible, it's also possible that the box sailed away to parts unknown and we'll never find it," Posey concluded glumly.

"That's not the worse possibility. What if someone else opens it? Even without the vials, a handwritten letter from Elvis has got to bring some money. A find like that would get a lot of publicity. That's probably all Doctor Ledbetter would need for verification. Might even up the price," Early May said.

"Oh dear. All those women wanting Elvis babies. Public awareness could definitely drive the price up. What a horrible idea! Let's not entertain that thought," Miss Maple pleaded.

"I'm more worried about what a direct hit could do to Elvis' energy field. There is no telling how long it would take him to recover. Assuming that he can mold his disembodied form together again. I just hope his scattered force is not a permanent condition." Kat blinked her eyes trying to fight back tears.

"Well, you can't die twice." Early May observed.

"I wonder if it feels as though you do." Posey muttered caustically.

"My notion is that Elvis merged with the atmosphere, just as he said he would. He adapts quickly. Remember the instant clothes?" Miss Maple suggested soothingly. Comforted by the thought, the women nodded in hopeful agreement.

The disharmony of wailing air abruptly abated. Diminishing rain was all that could be heard in the sudden near silence. The radio was dead, batteries exhausted. Relative quiet was somehow more ominous than the recently raging storm.

"Do you suppose it's safe to go upstairs and see if there is an upstairs?" Early May ventured.

"I'm game," Posey agreed. She hurried toward the stairs. Early May blocked her path.

"I'm going first. It was my idea and I'm closer to the stairs." Early May announced emphatically.

"Whatever," Posey shrugged, paused, then darted around Early May and bounded up the stairs.

"That's not fair!" Early May shouted in disgust.

"Who ever told you life was fair?" Posey shouted over her shoulder as she rushed to the top of the steps.

"I suppose children must play. I doubt that I could out run you if you gave me a very long head start," Miss Maple said to Kat with a smile.

"We don't have to play Posey's games. She just likes to show the results of working out at the gym. We'll just take our time. I'm not really anxious to find out what's happened."

"Yes, not knowing is better than finding bad news," Miss Maple agreed.

A few minutes past while footsteps continued to creak on the overhead boards, tracing the paths of the two upstairs explorers. Minutes expanded, until at last Posey called down from the basement door.

"Okay you scaredy-cats. There doesn't appear to be any damage on this floor. Early May's gone up to the second to see if the roof is still attached. The good news is that the fence is completely knocked down. If we hurry, we can check on the barn before the news media and cops get there."

Miss Maple and Kat arrived on the first floor at the same time Early May descended from upstairs.

"There doesn't appear to be as much as a water leak anywhere on the second floor. The only damage to the property seems to be the blown down fence," Early May reported.

"Yeah, I saw that. Looks like an open invitation to go check the damage at Graceland," Posey observed.

"Before company arrives. There is no need for you to go Miss Maple. We all don't need to get wet," Kat added.

"Why don't you turn on the TV? Elvis might turn up" Posey recommended.

Chapter Twenty

Heaven had opened the flood gates again. Sheets of rain cascaded from the sky while the women pushed forward toward the unknown. An outline of the barn could be seen in the distance. Its condition could not be determined. They maneuvered toward the structure on a path strewn with uprooted trees, large broken limbs mixed with various forms of debris. Finally, they approached the clearing.

"If Elvis was sucked up through that big hole in the roof, we might have just an unfriendly trio for a welcoming committee," Posey proclaimed. "Any idea how we're going to handle this?"

"We're just neighbors that are curious about the damage," Kat answered.

"You really think they'll buy that. Sounds like a wrong time, wrong place set up to me," Early May complained

"If you've got a better idea, let's hear it," Kat snapped.

Abruptly the rain became a sprinkle then eased to a complete stop. The barn door opened and a dazed Hercules started out the entrance. His appearance was disheveled as he took several unsteady steps into the yard. His eyes immediately began to search the area. They narrowed as the women came into his view. He stared blankly as they approached.

Kat called out, "Hi! We're neighbors. The news said the barn was hit. We thought we'd check it out before the media arrives. I'm sure they'll have police assigned to keep out intruders."

"We promise not to take anything if you'll let us look around," Posey added.

"What's the damage inside?" Early May asked.

"Just that big hole," Hercules answered, pointing toward the roof.

"Was anybody hurt? You look a little shook up," Posey inquired.

A dazed Hercules slowly answered. "It was the damnedest thing. One second I'm holding this black metal box. The next second it's sailing up to the ceiling and on out the top. My body felt like I'd stuck my finger in a light socket." He began to abruptly shake his head in an effort to clear his thoughts.

"I saw you looking around as we came up. Is the box what you're looking for? Maybe we can help you find it," Early May offered.

"He's got friends that will help him do that. I don't think you women need to be back here," A large man called from the barn door. Another man of equal size joined him by the doorway.

"We don't need to be back here? And exactly who are you?" Early May countered.

"We just want to look around," Kat hastily interjected. Flustered she continued as she pointed to Early May. "She use to work with Elvis' animals. We were just wondering if any of the horses got hurt."

"Hell, all of Elvis animals are as dead as he is. How long has it been since you handled his critters?"

Early May nervously fingered her ponytail. Her eyes flashed with open hostility toward the man by the barn door.

"It was damned sure before they died."

Hercules was the only one of the threesome that laughed.

"You the gal who worked for that old drunk, Doc Belle?" The man in the doorway narrowed his eyes while he scanned Early May. A faint smile slipped onto his lips.

Silent alarm bells rang simultaneously in the women's minds.

Stupid. Stupid. Stupid. Kat chastised herself silently. Why had she said anything about Early May?

The derogatory mention of Doc Belle triggered Early May's natural redheaded temperament. "Who the hell are you guys and what gives you the right to be asking us questions? If you must know, I was the nutritionist Elvis kept on staff to make sure the animals ate right."

"Really? From the looks of you, you've forgotten everything you knew," The front man replied sarcastically.

Early May had been a sprinter in school. She was still fast. She also had four older brothers. Fighting was a way of life for her. Her first blow broke the man's nose. He staggered a look of disbelief on his face. The next punch landed on his eye. It began to swell immediately. Hercules stepped between them, grasped Early May's arms, holding them over her head with one hand. His other arm circled her waist drawing her toward him. He whispered in her ear. "The man's got no taste in woman. I'm Herc, and I like big ladies with fire in their eyes."

"Wait a minute, damn it!" shouted Posey. "All we want to do is look around. Security is going to be all over us any minute now and we'll lose our chance."

Posey marched passed the stunned men and through the barn door. Kat was right behind her. Early May reluctantly pulled away from the stranger's embrace and joined them.

The interior of the barn wasn't damaged except for the rip in the ceiling directly above a water-filled hole in the floor. This time Elvis had definitely left the building.

Distant police sirens could be heard moving closer. Posey turned to exit the barn.

"Let's get out of here. I don't feel like answering a lot of questions."

Kat nodded in agreement as she followed her. Early May lingered near the back stalls.

"Come on Early May. There's nothing to do now but go back to the house and wait," Kat called to her.

"Exactly what would you be waiting for?" asked the battered, broken nosed man. He deliberately blocked their exit.

"Are you sure you want to be here when the police arrive?" Early May asked sarcastically as she approached her recent victim. "You haven't explained what you boys were up to. Would the cops be interested I wonder?" Her surprise victory fight made her cocky.

"You and me've got unfinished business. This is not the end of it." The man's voice trembled with barely suppressed anger as he glared at Early May.

"Anytime you feel up to it big boy," Early May challenged.

"Come on Tony, let's get out of here," Herc suggested as he entered the barn. "We need to get this equipment back." He hastily retrieved the jackhammer then started in the direction of the white van. He took a dozen or so steps, turned his head, then with a half smile, winked at Early May.

"Pick up those shovels, Ernie," Tony barked to the other man. He hissed a promise to Early May when he passed her.

"We will meet again."

"Hurry up Tony. Those police sirens are getting closer," Herc urgently shouted.

"This aint over yet," Tony's voice deepened to a low growl.

"Maybe next time you ought to let your buddies help," Early May called after him.

Tony ignored her but Herc turned his head again and laughed as the bulky trio walked hurriedly away. The women watched them disappear into the backyard where the van was parked.

Just as they started to follow in that direction, squad cars pulled into the area surrounding the barn. The police began to erect barricades with yellow, police line DO NOT CROSS, streamers attached. Television crews began to arrive just before the barricades were in place. They parked haphazardly on the lawn and began darting everywhere unloading their equipment.

Kat, Posey and Early May escaped during the confusion. They simply walked away.

Chapter Twenty-one

The wet, bedraggled women eagerly entered the warm, dry house. Miss Maple was perched on the edge of her seat watching the television.

"Any Elvis sightings?" Posey called from the door.

"I'm afraid not. The reception is just horrid. Still and all I managed to understand was that the equipment barn was the one demolished. How was the horse barn?"

"The only damage was a big opening in the roof. However, our little black box was sucked up through it. It's out there somewhere just waiting to be discovered," Kat reported glumly.

"My goodness! How do you know that?"

"We had a little discussion with the diggers. A guy named Herc had it in his hands then it just spiraled up and away," Early May answered.

"I wonder if Elvis was present when that happened," Miss Maple mused.

"Who knows where Elvis was or is," Posey replied.

"I'm beginning to feel uneasy about spending much more time here. Now it seems rather pointless anyway," Miss Maple sighed.

"I agree. We're going to have to find another place to hole up. I need to get some dry clothes, at the same time I'll be able to check on things in Tupelo. Y'all can get my phone number from the operator. I'm the only Early May Pruitt. It'll take less than two hours to get back here if anything turns up," Early May announced as she picked up her big purse and headed toward the front door.

"Why don't you plan to spend the night at my place, then leave refreshed in the morning. In any event, take my card. You could ring us when you arrive in Tupelo," Miss Maple suggested.

Early May hesitated. Miss Maple smiled. "It's all right dear, you may call collect. We just want to keep in touch."

Early May took the card from the older woman's outstretched hand. "I am pretty bushed. You got anything dry I can wear?"

"As a matter of fact, my late father was a rather large man. I still have some of his night shirts stored away. I've also been thinking, there's no point in you ladies staying at that motel when my house will accommodate all of us.

"That's a very generous offer. I do feel Elvis would prefer us to stay together," Kat agreed.

"Assuming Elvis has managed to stay together himself," Posey added.

"We won't dwell on that possibility. Besides you all need to get out of your wet garments before you catch your death of cold. We will just stop by the motel for your belongings."

Chapter Twenty-two

The hypnotic whirring of the ceiling fan was the last thing Early May remembered before she sank into a Rip Van Winkle slumber. It was the first sound she heard as she struggled to awaken. The lids of her eyes refused to cooperate as she willed them to open. Never mind, I'll just sleep a tad longer, she thought kicking the covers off. She spread her arms and legs akimbo to fully embrace the breeze.

Downstairs the other women gathered in the kitchen. Miss Maple was unloading the dryer. Kat and Posey sat on opposite sides of a small table.

"Do you think we ought to wake her?" Kat fretted.

"Well, her clothes are ready, Miss Maple replied."I'm glad she left them in the bathroom so that I could ready them for her."

"I think when she gets a whiff of lunch her nose will lead her down here. Miss Maple, you're going to way too much trouble," Posey protested.

"Nonsense! The chicken is almost thawed. It will be delightful to cook for someone other than myself. Our big meal was always around noon. We'd have something light in the evening for supper. Besides, toast and coffee is not much of a breakfast to my notion."

"If you insist on feeding us, what we can do to help?" Kat implored. "I'll not have you doing it all yourself."

"Certainly dear, you can start by peeling the potatoes and there are vegetables to cut up for salad."

It was nearly one o'clock when the aroma of frying chicken wafted upstairs to twitch Early May's taste buds. Her mouth began to salivate as her eyes finally opened.

I've died and gone to heaven. Early May smiled to herself.

Abruptly her reverie was interrupted by the jarring sound of Posey's voice calling from the bottom of the stairs.

"Are you ever going to get up? The food is almost on the table. I know you don't want to miss a meal but you better hurry or I'll eat your share."

Early May bounded out of the bed. "No you don't! I'm on my way."

The lunch had been southern fried delicious. The only thing missing was a cobbler of some kind, Early May thought as she backed her car down the driveway. It proved difficult to steer with a strong pull to the right and a decided uneven lurch. Early May turned off the motor and disgustedly got out to check the problem.

"Damn it!" Early May shouted. The back tire was totally deflated. She started for the trunk, and then remembered. Damn, damn, damn, her thoughts screamed as she kicked the useless tire. How long have I been meaning to get that spare fixed? Calling a garage was her best solution.

Chapter Twenty-three

Deepening, late, afternoon shadows lengthened as the sun eased lower in the west before Early May actually headed for Tupelo.

I was bound to run out of luck for not plugging that hole in the spare sooner, she fumed.

Lost in thought she failed to notice the ensuing silver pickup until a few miles south of Memphis on Highway 78. She grew increasingly apprehensive until the truck disappeared at the Holly Springs Exit. Her sigh of relief was short-lived. Just as she began to feel comfortable, the truck reappeared, speeding past her. The driver immediately slowed to pull in front of her compact car.

Who the hell? More angry than anxious, Early May immediately pulled out then maneuvered along the driver's side. Tony's swollen eyes glared back at her. He looked ready for a rematch.

Instinctively, she eased her foot off the gas pedal, slowly touched the brake then pulled in behind him. Suddenly, a head popped out of the passenger side of the truck and turned toward her.

Herc!

Could he possibly be her deliverance? Early May wondered if he had felt the same stirrings, that sudden rush of desire she encountered amid the confusion by the barn. He'd said he liked big women and had sounded like he meant it.

What a time to be thinking about getting laid. Early May shook her head in self disgust. Still, she wished that his bruised buddy was someplace else nursing his wounds. As long as Tony was around she didn't dare go home.

The prospect of out driving him wasn't an option. Where could she find quick help off this highway? Some place with people....

The Mall!

Mingling with a crowd would at least slow them down. It might deter them from committing any serious damage before some form of help arrived. Also, it might give Herc time to decide how much he really liked big women. Early May slammed the accelerator to the floor board.

Where was Elvis when you needed him?

Her car edged passed them to briefly take the lead. High speed tag continued down the highway for several miles. Tony toyed with the lead, relinquished it briefly, only to recapture it again. The turn off to Tupelo was fast approaching.

If I can just get him to pull ahead when we get close to an exit, I can turn off. He'll have to go to the next exit to turn around. That will buy me a little time. Maybe enough to get to the shopping center, Early May theorized.

Almost concurrent with those thoughts, Tony decided to show off. He accelerated past her, and then noticed the approaching exit too late to slow for a possible turn.

Early May felt exhilarated as she slammed on the brakes, and then guided the small car off the highway. She swiftly took the east road toward the closest place where there would be people.

Her euphoria was short-lived.

Tony did not go to the next exit. Instead he hit the brakes hard, tires smoking, made an U-turned in the middle of the highway. Game time was over.

Early May quickly picked up their return in her rearview mirror. The image magnified until the reality was traveling beside her. Herc gave her an uncomfortable smile as the truck momentarily matched her speed then pulled back directly behind her. Immediately the huge pickup began to pound her car. The jolts increased in intensity. The compact was no match for the monster.

Each ram seemed to jar her whole being until finally her battered car careened into the ditch that skirted the road. The explosion of breaking glass and crumbling metal were the last sounds Early May heard as her limp, queen size body was flung like a rag doll, over the now useless steering wheel.

Chapter Twenty-four

"I'm afraid that there is something dreadfully wrong," Miss Maple fretted as she put the phone back in its cradle.

It had been easy to get Early May's number from Information. However nearly four hours after she left Memphis, there was still no answer to the ring.

"Two vanished, three to go. Our little group grows smaller," Posey observed cryptically.

"I feel so totally helpless," Kat lamented.

"Yeah, Early May may not be able to pull her Mohammed Ali if she runs into hardware trouble," Posey added.

Miss Maple looked confused.

"Fights, guns and knives," Posey enlightened.

"If Elvis were only here. He could lay all our fears to rest in just moments. I'm so afraid for the dear boy. My fervent desire is that nothing irreparable has happened to him."

"I wish that we had some inkling that he is alive."

"He's not alive, Kat. And to quote Early May, they can't kill you twice."

"Oh, you know what I mean. That his spirit is still able to contact us."

"I wonder if we should try to contact him, Miss Maple suggested.

"How?"

"I have an old Ouija Board."

The two younger women exchanged incredulous looks.

Miss Maple continued. "My mother was a dabbler in spiritualism."

"I've never trusted those board games. You either end up with gibberish or earthbound spirits," Posey retorted.

"I've gotten some pretty interesting readings in the past," Kat inserted.

"Your subconscious is a very interesting place," Posey laughed.

"You don't know that it was my subconscious. I could have picked up someone," Kat replied huffily.

"Your pick-up skills have never been in question, coupled with your unique grasp of the paranormal...."

"What exactly does that mean?" Kat interrupted.

Miss Maple attempted to deflect the approaching argument.

"My mother always said if you go toward the project with love in your heart, love is what you receive. I sat with her many times and we never had a bad experience," Miss Maple paused and looked at the two women. "Shall I go get the board?"

"At least we'll feel as though we're doing something," Kat agreed.

"Why not. How much worse can it get? No, Kat, don't answer that. I'll just put a little love in my heart and send out signals of white light."

"Then it's settled. We will ask the Ouija for help. I know exactly where it is." Miss Maple left to retrieve the board from its hiding place in the back of the hall closet.

She returned with the planchette and the rectangular piece of smooth wood with the Sun and Moon in the upper corners. Under the Sun was YES. Under the Moon the word NO. Two rows of the alphabet spanned across the middle with numbers 1 through 0 below them. GOOD-BYE, underlined near the bottom, was its final message.

"Ladies, let's go into the dining room where we can move our chairs together," Miss Maple suggested. "I'll dim the lights and burn a few candles. The spirits seem to be drawn to their glow. I have some crystals that we can place on the table for added energy."

Once they were situated with the chairs in a circle, their knees touching. Miss Maple made another suggestion.

"It has always worked best for me when two people place their hands on the instrument. The messages seemed clearer. Who shall go first?"

"I leave that honor to you girls. I'll busy myself with sending the white light and loving thoughts," Posey quipped.

"If you aren't going to take this seriously, we might as well not do it," Kat snapped.

"Posey dear, we do need your help. We all must concentrate if we are to get the best results."

"For you, Miss Maple, I'll give it a sincere try," Posey responded.

"Thank you, Posey. I appreciate your input. Now Kat let us place our hands lightly on the pointer. Miss Maple hesitated. "I wonder if we shouldn't just try to find someone on the other side that is willing to make a connection with us."

"Not just ask for Elvis? That should certainly give us more of a chance for a response," Kat concurred.

"Yeah, maybe one of the disembodied spirits saw Elvis take that last joy ride and knows where we can locate him," Posey added.

"I hope the location is all in one place. I hate to think of his energy being scattered beyond recovery," Kat lamented.

"We must try to refrain from entertaining those kinds of thoughts. Shall we begin by holding hands, and bowing our head in a moment of silent prayer?" Without waiting for a reply, Miss Maple reached for a hand on either side. She enfolded them in a soft embrace.

After the hushed benediction, Kat and Miss Maple placed their fingers lightly on the planchette. Miss Maple whispered, "Is anyone there?"

A somber silence enveloped the atmosphere and gently surrounded the trio. The pointer began to slowly move. It came to rest on YES.

"Are you Elvis?" Miss Maple questioned.

NO.

"Do you know Elvis?"

The pointer meandered across the board, then paused sequentially at K, I, N, G.

"Ask if it knows where his majesty is," Posey interjected impatiently. "Wait! We may need to record this. I saw a pad and pen over by the phone." Posey jumped up to retrieve them. When she returned Miss Maple quietly asked the question concerning Elvis's whereabouts.

The marker immediately began to glide over the alphabet, pausing briefly over certain letters. Kat and

Miss Maple spoke each selection aloud while Posey recorded the information. Finally the movement stopped on GOOD-BYE.

"Let's see what we have. First letter E. Next V." Posey continued to call out each consecutive symbol until she reached the end. She shook her head in disgust. "Just like I predicted. Gibberish."

"Perhaps I can decipher the message. Sometimes the spirits communicate in a kind of shorthand. I was rather good at translating when I was a girl." Miss Maple began to carefully verbalize the inscription on the pad. "E v ...wh... er" Suddenly she gasped as she recognize the connection. "Everywhere. He's everywhere. OH, that poor, dear, boy."

"What do you suppose that really means?" Kat was truly alarmed.

"That your scattered image was probably prophetic. Ask for clarification," Posey suggested.

"Or if there is anyway to contact him," Kat added hopefully.

"Yes, that would probably be the best way to proceed." Miss Maple agreed.

She and Kat returned their hands to the planchette while she asked the question aloud. "Can we make direct contact with Elvis?" The instrument began to move immediately toward the edge of the board. It stopped when it reached YES.

"How?" Miss Maple continued.

The pointer began to dance wildly around the board. Neither Kat nor Miss Maple was in control. Finally, when the energy diminished, it stopped briefly on S before proceeding slowly toward the second letter A. The selection continued for a few more moments, then halted on Good-bye. Miss Maple began to sound out each syllable. The lettering read saahts. Finally she intoned "Say ants." She repeated it several times before excitedly arriving at her conclusion. "Séance! They want us to conduct a séance."

"Do you know how to hold one?" Kat asked.

"I certainly don't," Posey replied quickly.

"Mother had some spiritualist books on the subject. I believe they are still stored in the attic. I'll go see if I can find them," Miss Maple answered as she rose and left the room.

"I'm not sure I want to try to contact the dead. There is no telling whose bones we'll rattle," Posey grumbled.

"I'm for anything that will help us make contact with Elvis."

"You would be."

"I don't know why you have to be so disagreeable."

"Let me see if I can come up with a reason. Could it be that we have traveled a long way, with nothing to show for our efforts? Or perhaps I'm a little testy from my recent near rendezvous with a Tennessee twister. Then there was that delightful stroll in the drenching rain, not to mention the lovely people we met. Furthermore, our spiritual adviser has taken flight and we are left with no clue to our next move. The most inspired rational is a séance, which none of us know how to conduct."

"Miss Maple has gone to get a book."

"Indeed. And you feel confident that we will be able to make contact with Elvis based on the instructions from a book?"

"I feel that we should at least try."

Posey shook her head wearily, then propped her elbows on her lap and rested her face in her palms. The silence remained unbroken until Miss Maple returned with a large black book in her hands.

"I feel certain this is the correct publication. I found the word séance in the Index. Would you read the instructions out loud dear? My eyes tire so easily." Miss Maple held out the book to Kat.

Kat took the volume, scanned the index for the page. She began to read. "Prepare the room with comfortable chairs around a table. Create the proper inviting atmosphere by placing fresh flowers, spiritual objects, crystals, candles. Utilize anything that will enhance the ambiance and energy of the area.

"Oh, I just picked some lovely roses this morning. The last pretty ones for awhile I believe. They are in a vase by the sink in the kitchen." Miss Maple remembered.

"I'll get them." Posey hurried toward the kitchen. She quickly returned with an assortment of pink and red flowers in a Waterford crystal vase. She placed them in the center of the table. When she sat down, Kat continued reading.

"Join hands in a circle while prayerfully blending your separate forces into one entity. Dedicate this space in time to God and the world of spirits. In your mind's eye, visualize the room being filled with the white light of protection. Sit quietly. Take several calming, deep breaths and become as still as possible."

"Sounds like the beginning of a meditation," Posey observed.

"Reaching the Alpha level is the initial process for both I believe. Do continue Kat," Miss Maple instructed.

"Ask your spirit guides to join you for additional protection. Pause while you silently feel their arrival. You might request a sign of their presence. This may take the form of a word or sensation. Allow enough time to tune into the vibration."

"When you feel at ease, send out your thoughts to the spirit world, asking them to blend their power with yours. At the moment you sense a spirit trying to make contact, proceed by saying, Greetings. Extend an invitation to come into your light or aura. With eyes closed, concentrate until you sense their emotions and images as a part of you. Receive their message. They may manifest as an apparition or simply a shadow form. Surround them with thoughts of love before asking your questions. Listen with an open heart to the replies.

When the session is concluded, send out a prayer to the spirits that have come. Then again see the white light filling the room, cleansing every particle, every space."

Kat looked totally perplexed as she closed the book. She searched Miss Maple's face hopefully for a sign of understanding. Miss Maple stared at her hands in her lap, as if unable to raise her eyes. Posey's sarcasm broke the silence.

"Goodness, is that all? Imagine me thinking this would be difficult."

Chapter Twenty-five

Early May felt careful hands on her aching body. She kept her eyes closed and pretended to still be unconscious. If she wasn't awake she couldn't answer questions. The big hands were gentle as they slid under her body and pulled her from the car.

"That's right, Baby. You just keep on pretending," Herc whispered in her ear as he pulled her close to his chest. "I think she must have took a hard hit to the head," he shouted to Tony, who sat fuming in the truck.

Tony jerked opened the door, swung his legs sideways in the seat. "Hell, you'll fall for anything. Throw her in the back and git in with her so she don't jump out." He abruptly stepped down as Herc passed. His eyes tightened as he watched Herc carefully place Early May's body on the rolls of tarp that covered the truck bed, and then climbed in beside her.

"You damn well better not git any ideas about helping her. You don't know the Boss as well as I do. What he'd do to you wouldn't make that piece of tail worth it." Tony climbed back into the cab of the truck, forcefully pulling the door shut beside him.

Herc picked up Early May's head and gingerly placed it in his lap just as Tony gunned the truck back onto the road. He held his face close to her ear and whispered, "Just tell him where that damned book is that he's after. I'll make sure he don't harm you anymore. You hurtin' bad now?"

Early May slowly half raised her lids and found Herc's concerned blue eyes only inches away. They were searching her face and head for signs of injury. A large red spot on her forehead was growing into a golf ball size lump. Herc brushed it with his lips.

"I'm ALL hurt...and that kiss won't work," Early May managed to mutter, turning her face away.

"I'm not workin' anything. You'll see," Herc replied. The truck created a piercing rush of wind as it zoomed back on the highway that consumed all other sounds, including Early May's involuntary moans.

Minutes stretched into eternity as Early May's battered body jolted with each uneven bump in the road before the truck finally slowed off the highway. It pulled into the parking lot of an inadequately lit, dilapidated, cottage-type motor inn. A VACANT sign hung in the dingy window. A tattered OPEN sign dangled lop-sided on the door. Tony hurried in that direction.

When he disappeared inside, Herc cautiously tilted Early May's face toward him. "You're going to have to trust me," he pleaded.

"I'm not exactly in a position of choice," Early May groaned as she tried to sit up. Herc wrapped his arms under her then pulled her upright against him. She stifled an outcry of pain.

"We need to get you to a emergency room," Herc worried.

"I'm not sure my sparring partner will agree to that. Your friend and I aren't chummy, remember?"

"He's sure as hell not my friend. I never saw him until yesterday. This was supposed to be just slightly illegal breaking and entering. They needed some extra beef for a heavy job."

"How did you get involved in something so stupid?"

"That other guy that was with us is my ignorant cousin Ernie. I don't like him much either, but I needed extra cash. He promised this was quick, easy money so as I could fix my truck. He was the one that was suppose to come with Tony, but I talked him into lettin' me come in his place. He's easy to put a scare into, so I knew he'd just let Tony do what he wanted with you."

"And why would you care what kind of mess he'd make out of me?"

Herc smiled. "I told you. I like big women. Particularly pretty ones."

"I'm sure you could find prettier ones in a lot less trouble. Do you have any idea the predicament you've gotten into?" Early May asked. She was genuinely curious about the depth of his involvement. She desperately wanted to believe him.

"I just know we're looking for some kind of book and some missing files. If you got 'um, give 'um up. I don't know much about the guy I'm workin' for except he's a mean S.O.B."

"You best do as the man says. Calling the Boss mean don't begin to describe him. I'm a real nice man when you compare us." Tony had returned, dangling a motel key in front of him as he walked to the side of the truck bed.

"We can do this easy but I kind of hope you make it hard." Tony's mangled face twisted into a perverse smile.

Rebellion masked Early May's fear as she determinedly set upright and screamed, partially with pain. "I don't have anything useful to you, you low-life piece of trash. Without the black box, none of us have anything."

"And what's it worth...with the black box?" The question rang with nasty implication.

"You telling me you all found that box?" Despite the belligerent tone, Early May's lower lip began to tremble involuntarily. She looked at Herc to make certain her fears were justified. She didn't like what she saw.

Chapter Twenty-six

The three women sat holding hands atop the dining room table. In the center, several partially burned candles blazed, illuminating the assortment of various sized crystals scattered in a loose circle around the interior objects on the table. The roses seemed to sink down in the vase, not wilted, but energy spent. The séance seekers reflected a similar physical strain as they held their uncomfortable vigil.

"No sign can not be a good sign," Posey observed as she pulled her hands away and straightened her shoulders. "I think an hour of deadly quiet is about all I'm willing to invest."

"I'm becoming rather fatigued myself," Miss Maple admitted, lightly rubbing her freed hands together.

Kat hunched her shoulders toward her ears then rolled her head, first toward the right then reversed. "Well, we're obviously doing something wrong. Either that, or Elvis has traveled beyond our ability to make contact."

"Perhaps if we retired early for the evening, a good night's rest would refresh us enough to make another try in the morning," Miss Maple suggested.

"That is an excellent idea," Posey agreed. She turned and smiled at Kat. "Besides, Elvis seems to like finding you in bed."

"That's right! He did say he could appear in my dreams if it was important."

Miss Maple spoke as she rose slowly from her chair. "Surely this interval is meaningful enough for contact. I don't know what we'll do without his assistance. I suggest we withdraw, pray for guidance and see in what direction we are led."

Mutually grateful to end the evening's efforts, the women separated to their previously selected bedrooms.

Sleep proved tricky as Kat tossed and turned on the unfamiliar bed. The musty smell of stale linens invaded her nostrils while the sound of creaky slat boards that supported the mattress springs sounded with every movement. Deprived of her sleep tapes, the minutes ticked loudly in her mind's clock. Hoping for a fresh breeze to move the stale air, she slipped out of bed and tried to open the window.

Stuck!

This is impossible. This room is so stuffy I can't breathe. Every time I turn I make enough noise to wake the dead. At that thought, Kat laughed out loud. If only that were true. She sighed as she reluctantly turned back toward the bed.

Elvis lay there waiting for her. Well, he wasn't all there. Sort of like the first time he'd appeared. Kat responded with a cry of delight as she quickly headed in his direction. She flung herself in total abandonment toward his reclined figure. The impact caused several slats to immediately dislodge, sending one side of the mattress and springs clattering to the floor. Kat landed face down on her pillow and rumbled covers.

"Good heavens! I've squashed him out of existence," Kat exclaimed after discovering he wasn't beneath her.

"No, darlin', I managed to reluctantly escape your hunk of burning love. My energy level is pretty low for any kind of connection right now." Elvis's hazy figure stood in front of the window Kat had attempted to open.

"Elvis you look..." Kat struggled for a description.

"Yeah, I know I must look a little washed out. But you could say I've been through the wringer. Haven't been able to recharge my vibes sufficiently."

"Exactly where have you been?"

"Doing business with a flash?" He seemed to be smiling.

"No, really. Did you find the box? Do you have it?"

"Yes and no."

Exasperated, Kat fumed. "Are you going to explain or play games?"

"I thought you liked games."

"If you're in a game-playing mood, why didn't you show up at the séance?"

"I was there. Just couldn't seem to make much of an impression. You all were so busy concentrating; I couldn't get your attention. Dividing what little energy I've got apparently put out a pretty puny signal."

"Oh, Elvis, I don't know what we're going to do if you're too weak to help. Early May disappeared this afternoon on her way to Tupelo. We're all afraid something has happened to her. She had a little confrontation with those thugs you saw at the barn."

"I better go find her." His figure began to fade as he spoke.

"Wait! Is there anything we can do to help you?"

"You all can send me white light to help recharge my energy field."

"How do we do that?"

"Visualize the white light all around me, and then send it with love and a prayer."

"Is that all?"

"If your intention is pure, love is always enough."

"Can't you delay leaving until you're stronger? How can you help her in your condition?"

"I've got to try, darlin'."

"Please give me some answers before you leave." Kat was talking to empty space. The well-known voice spoke out of that darkness.

"Sorry sweet, but I can't let one of our warriors fight the battle alone."

Chapter Twenty-seven

Early May lay still on top of the faded blue chenille bedspread. Her arms and legs were tied in front of her with the same piece of rope. The already small room seemed further dwarfed by the three oversized occupants.

Tony stood by the open cabin door. "You damned well better be telling me the truth about that book being in your purse in the car. It won't take us that long to get back here. Our reunion will be more than a little painful if you're stupid enough to be lyin'."

Early May twisted her head for a defiant look at Tony. "You think I'd lay here like a roped cow waitin' to be slaughtered? Of course the damned thing is in my purse. Unless somebody's come along and stolen it." Her eyes shifted quickly to Herc, standing by the bed. Could he and would he help? And did it matter? The book didn't really contain anything they didn't already know. However, if they had the black box, they'd know she had notarized Elvis's letter of verification. That's the book that might give the additional proof that Elvis's note was authentic.

"She needs some lookin' after. Maybe I ought to stay here and keep an eye on her," Herc suggested.

"Who'd keep an eye on you?" Tony snarled. "Here." Tony fished in his pocket and pulled out a large crumpled, dirty handkerchief. "Gag her with this. I'll turn on the TV in case she makes some noise."

Herc rolled the cloth, then bent down to insert the restraint in Early May mouth. "Bite down," he whispered as he began to loosely tie the knot behind her head. He pulled it taunt as her teeth sank into the soiled fabric. From the front it looked to be securely bound.

"You tying it tight, right?" Tony demanded, as he played with the TV volume control.

"Look for yourself," Herc answered indifferently. He continued to feign unconcern as he walked toward Tony.

"Well, it don't matter much. The old coot behind the front desk is near deaf. I doubt that he'd hear a bomb going off." Tony turned his attention toward Early May. "You be real good while we're gone or I might have to test that old man's hearing when we get back."

Early May listened for the sound of the departing truck before she spit out the soiled material. She easily wrestled it to her hairline then maneuvered herself to the side of the bed. She shook her head until the gag fell on the floor.

Now what? The television was blaring loud enough to drown out any sound she might make. Her hands and feet were bound so close together that she wouldn't be able to walk if she rolled off the bed on to the carpet. Over an hour of being verbally tormented and threatened by Tony left her so mentally depleted that she couldn't think clearly, much less formulate a plan.

Reverberating static broke through her thoughts. The TV picture had disappeared into wavy horizontal lines. Barely audible over the crackling discord, a voice quivered across the airwaves.

"Early May, don't worry. It's nearly over now."

Unsure of what she'd heard, Early May responded in a hushed tone. "Elvis, is that you? What do you mean it's nearly over? Am I going to die?"

Elvis' chuckle was loud enough to be distinctly heard. His voice began to sound more vital.

"No, sweetheart. Just give them whatever they want."

Early May bent her body forward then tilted her head toward the television. "I can't see you!" she shrieked.

"My energetic field is on low voltage. I'm trying to recharge it. I've got just about enough juice left to scan your body and maybe lift some of the pain."

"You haven't just given up, have you? You're not just going to let them have your...popsicles."

"Trust me and stall them as long as you can. Take them to your house and give them everything Doc Belle sent you."

"Have they got the black box?"

Elvis laughed. "Yeah, for all the good it's doing them. It kind of got struck by lightening. Sort of fused it together. They haven't decided how to crack it without damaging the contents. Of course, they don't know whether the contents are fried or not."

"Are they?" Early May worried.

"I can still see something in it, but I can't quite make out the condition. Not that it matters much. By the way, there was a big guy there that was awfully eager to come after you. Good clean aura about him. Seemed genuinely concerned."

Early May attempted a smile. "That's Herc."

"Well, give them what they want, but take your time. The longer you can drag it out the stronger my vibrations will become. And the more help I can be to you. However, if they push you too hard, go ahead and give in. I don't think the big fellow will let anything serious happen to you. In the meantime, I'll get you some help."

"Hurry, I'm hurtin' all over," Early May pleaded.

Elvis quickly scanned her body for serious injury.

"Nothing seems to be broken. Just some bad bruises. Close your eyes."

Early May readily complied. A shivering sensation swept though her, starting at the crown of her head, descending downward, then out the soles of her feet. The tingling deepened until the pain departed.

So had Elvis.

Chapter Twenty-eight

Kat laid on the bed, stunned and unsure what direction to take after Elvis' unexpected appearance. Were Posey and Miss Maple asleep? Even so, this startling event certainly justified interruption. Posey would assuredly want immediate disclosure.

Kat rose as quietly as possible and tiptoed out the door, down the hall. She knocked softly on Posey's door.

"No, my bed is not anymore comfortable than yours, Kat."

Kat opened the door and slipped in. She spoke in an exaggerated whisper.

"Elvis showed up."

Posey sat up, immediately attentive. "Was that his noisy entrance I heard a little while back?"

Kat nodded. "Actually it was me jumping on him. I knocked some slats out."

"And what did your unbridled enthusiasm do to Mr. Presley?"

"He managed to escape to the window."

"Ah, the one who got away? Precisely where is King Presley now?"

"He's gone to help Early May, except he's so weak I don't see how he's going to..."

"Wait. Let's go to the kitchen for a nightcap. I want you to start at the beginning and tell me straight through."

Kat and Posey sat at the ornately carved Maplewood table. The teakettle began to whistle softly. Kat jumped up before the sound could reach its maximum level. Simultaneously, Posey retrieved a couple of new herbal tea bags from the cupboard.

"Too bad there wasn't any liquor. Oh well, let's let Miss Maple sleep. From all you've told me, there doesn't seem a reason to wake her."

"You're right. However, I don't think we can start praying too soon." Kat reached for the steaming teacup. "He and Early May are both going to need some psychic protection."

"I would hate to be out there relying on us for salvation."

"We're all they've got, so I guess we beat nothing."

"Barely."

They sipped their second cup of tea in silent reflection. The faint sound of light footsteps caught their attention just as Miss Maple appeared in the doorway.

"It seems I'm not the only one being deprived of sleep. I thought a cup of chamomile might be pleasant. It looks as though you ladies had the same idea." Miss Maple walked toward the cupboard as she continued tying the sash to her robe.

"I hope we didn't wake you," Kat replied.

"Oh, no dear. I'm a rather nocturnal creature. The older I get, the less I want to sleep. When you add in my growing concern for Elvis...." Miss Maple's voice trailed off.

"He made an appearance," Kat interrupted.

"You might have heard the crash," Posey added ruefully.

"Is he all right? Where is he now? No, wait until I finish preparing my tea. I want to give the explanation my full attention."

Miss Maple sat immersed in silence concentration while Kat reviewed Elvis's brief visit.

"Now he wants us to transmit white light to him so he'll be able to help Early May," Kat concluded.

"Then I suggest we conduct a prayer vigil in the parlor." Miss Maple rose without waiting for a reply, and then strode purposely toward the front of the house.

Miss Maple entered the parlor, turned on a lamp then seated herself in the center of the large beige brocade sofa. "I suggest you ladies seat yourselves on each side. We can join hands while we offer silent prayers."

This is where Elvis found them, their heads bowed, eyes closed. His shadowy outline hovered slightly above the floor in front of them. Quietly, while his form began to gain substance, he watched over them. When he became clearly visible, he spoke.

"Thank you, ladies for your loving petition. I feel a strong vitality flowing directly into my spirit. You girls are a God sent," he announced enthusiastically.

Three pair of eyes flashed opened.

"Dear boy, I'm so relieved to see you...all together," Miss Maple enthused.

"You do look more filled out than a little while ago. Guess there is something to this prayer thing," Kat added.

"I am so delighted with your reappearance. Were you able to locate Early May?" Miss Maple inquired.

"Easy as a roller coaster ride."

"I guess you found her in the Fun House," Posey retorted.

"I doubt she'd call it that. She looks like she might have been on the bad end of a messy bumper car collision."

"Where is she..." Kat started.

"And what's happening to her?" Posey finished.

"The big boys caught up with her just as she got to Tupelo. Apparently they rammed her car off the road then took her to a beat-up old motel where they left her tied up while they went back to get her purse. They figure she's got useful information in it."

"How severe are her injuries?" Miss Maple inquired.

"She was pretty painfully bruised but no bones broken."

"I take it you have x-ray vision," Posey suggested sardonically.

"Something like that. I soothed her with some of Dr. Presley's instant remedy. She shouldn't be aching too much now."

"What can we do to help?" Miss Maple asked.

"Keep sending me those loving thought prayers and ask for a little angelic aid. Just in case I can't regroup enough to make a difference, in about an hour call the Mississippi Police and report a disturbance at Early May's house.

"Why wait?" Kat asked impatiently.

"I want the bad guys to get all the information she has."

"You're not making any sense. I thought our game plan was to keep everything away from them."

Elvis smiled.

"Different game. New rules."

"And we're the pawns, not the players since you seem disinclined to share," Posey added in mild irritation.

"You all are big time players, Posey. Just keep visualizing and sending me your collective energy. Nothing could be more helpful. I need that rejuvenating power when I go back to keep an eye on Early May."

"Don't go before you explain our sudden change of plans!" Kat insisted.

"Just trust me. Do as I say and it will all work out. I'll give you a complete update when I return."

Elvis' image rapidly faded into nothingness.

Chapter Twenty-nine

Early May lay listening for the sound of the returning truck. The pulse in her bound wrists and ankles began throb again just as the pain from the inflexible curve of her back radiated through every nerve. Giving in would be easy. Anything to end this agony. Finally, she heard the unmistakable crunch of tires on gravel, followed by the squeal of a sudden stop. Heavy metal doors slammed. Tony erupted into the room, shaking the ledger in his hand.

"This damned book is worthless!"

"That's what I tried to tell you," Early May retorted.

"Well, little lady, you just sealed your own fate," Tony made a menacing move toward the bed.

"Hold it, Tony!" Herc demanded as he entered the room. "For your own sake Early May, tell him what you know and I'll make the bastard leave you alone."

Tony reeled to face Herc. "So that's how it's going to be. I never did put much stock in you."

"I think the Boss would be more interested in gettin' the information than possibly being involved with beatin' up a woman. As I hear it, he's gettin' a little tired of your temper." Herc stepped around Tony and knelt beside the bed.

"Please Early May, let's just get this behind us," he pleaded.

Early May searched his earnest expression for traces of honesty. His guileless, blue eyes beseeched her trust while his powerful, big hands gently grazed the side of her cheek. Refusal would have been difficult under any circumstance. Luckily, giving in was the right thing to do.   Still, Early May stalled for time.

"Exactly what are you looking for?"

"I think you know without being told," Tony snarled.

"Everything I've got is at my house." Early May squirmed then moaned softly.

"Undo these ropes and I'll take you there."

"Why are you suddenly so eager to help?" Tony asked suspiciously.

"Because I'm sick of this whole mess. My wrists and ankles feel like they're on fire. I'll probably have a permanent hump in my back...and I need to pee."

Herc smiled as he immediately began to untie her. Tony started to speak but Herc's challenging glare stopped him. "I'm gettin' these ropes off her. When we go to her house your job will be over. You just take the stuff back and get your pay. Tell the Boss to give you mine too."

Tony looked undecided.

"...if on the other hand you figure you'd rather have pay back, than pay off, I can promise I'll be at least as tough an opponent as Early May."

The open cabin door suddenly slammed shut. The television blared, piercing the air with static.

Elvis was back!

Tony eyes widened then narrowed to slits as he immediately snapped off the television. He turned around to speak. The cabin door rattled against an unseen force, then burst open again.

"All right, let's get out of here. This place is beginning to give me the creeps."

Herc hastily finished untying Early May. He lifted her feet slightly and moved them to the side of the bed as he placed his arm around her back and gently pulled her upright. She struggled briefly with her balance then hobbled toward the bathroom. When she shut the door Herc turned to face Tony.

"I mean what I say, Tony. You best leave her alone. The Boss said no violence, remember?"

Tony sneered. "I remember he said to get the proof any way I had to. Without any commotion, if possible. I'm still not sure it's going to be possible. Can't trust your new girlfriend."

"You can trust me, and I promise you better make the right decision."

"Or what?"

Herc's features contorted into a fierce mask of barely controlled anger.

"Or I'll cut your balls off and let Early May wear them for earrings."

The motel door began to quiver. In an instant, the agitation increased until the door slammed shut. Simultaneously, the television snapped on. A sudden gust of wind immediately began to press against the outside with increased velocity until the door burst open again.

Tony decided it was time to leave.

Chapter Thirty

The drive to Early May's small white framed house took less than ten minutes.

"You better be telling the truth about living alone," Tony threatened as they parked the truck in the driveway.

"You think I'd want to involve anybody else? The only live thing inside is my cat. You might have to watch out for him. He's pretty mean."

Herc chuckled as he opened the door and helped Early May down from the cab.

Tony grasped Early May's purse from the seat as he jumped down from the driver's side. "You keep mouthing off and I'll give you a real sample of mean." He tossed her purse to her.

"Unless you want me to use your hard head as a ramming rod, you best find that house key in a hurry."

Early May easily found the guitar-shaped key ring in the bottom of her bag. The prickly return of circulation in her legs made walking awkward and slow. Tony bounded ahead of her. When he reach the porch, he turned back to hurry her.

Suddenly the door began to tremble behind him. He swiftly twisted around just as it burst open and slammed against the inside wall. Simultaneously the tremor spread to include the front porch while the intense vibration filled the air with unfamiliar surges. A visibly shaken Tony ran down the steps and pulled Early May up on the porch. Herc followed closely behind.

"Are you makin' this shit happen?" Tony demanded as he pushed her inside. "If you are you got to be some kind of witch."

Early May turned to face Tony with a half smile and hard eyes. "Could be. I'd be a mite more careful if I was you."

Herc look bewildered as he hesitantly entered the room. He noticed Killer the cat sitting petrified in the middle of the coffee table, his black fur sticking straight out, green eyes wide with horrified expectation.

"Your cat looks a tad upset," he said softly.

Early May immediately picked Killer up and started soothing him. "What's the matter with Mama's wittle boy? You tired of eating that ol' dry cat food?"

"Put that damned cat down and get me what we come here for," Tony growled impatiently.

"I'm feeding my cat first. If you are in such a hurry, go get it yourself. It's in a cardboard box on the top shelf in the front bedroom closet."

Tony started to object but Herc stepped between them, as Early May went into the kitchen.

"You heard her. You want it. Go get it."

"And take a chance on her running off?" Tony briskly maneuvered passed Herc into the kitchen. Just as he crossed the threshold a Graceland souvenir plate hanging on the wall crashed to the floor.

The abrupt noise terrified the already frightened Killer. He gave a piercing howl as he jumped from Early May's arms, ricocheted on to Tony chest before bounding to the floor and out the door. Early May deliberately ignored the shattered dish and the cat's behavior.

"Well I guess he wasn't as hungry as I thought."

"What the hell happened with that plate?" Tony pointed to the pieces on the floor. Early May glanced in that direction and shrugged her shoulders. "Must have been hung on a loose nail."

A loud rattle from the top of the refrigerator captured their attention. The ceramic Elvis head cookie jar seemed to glide to the edge tilt over until the hair lid fell to the floor. Early May nonchalantly began picking up the broken pieces. She turned to look up at Tony.

"I think it would be a good idea if you got what you came for and left. My house doesn't seem to like you."

"That's what I wanted when we got here. It was your idea to feed that damned cat."

"He doesn't seem to be all that hungry so we might as well get this business over with."

Early May left the fragmented glass hair on the kitchen counter before abruptly turning to walk in the direction of the bedroom. Herc gave her a quizzical look as she passed him. She smiled reassuringly. "I'm sure you won't mind getting that big box down for me."

"Sure thing." He readily replied. Visibly still bewildered, he headed in that direction immediately. The living room lights began to flicker as he passed through. When he disappeared into the hall a burst of dazzling blue white brilliance filled the area then immediately dimmed to a golden glow before fading into complete darkness. The erratic light show continued in no particular sequence.

"You best hurry it up." Tony nervously demanded.

Early May observed the inconsistent display with amusement. "Goodness! I wonder if I paid my electric bill."

Moments later Herc returned with the cardboard carton in his arms. The lights intensified their random functioning until Tony stepped forward and jerked the box from Herc.

"Everything better be in here or I'll be back," The slight quiver in Tony's voice contradicted his command.

"I don't think you'll be coming back," Herc answered firmly. At the same time the lights began to glow consistently.

"Besides, my house might get really upset next time," Early May added.

Before Tony could reply, the front door began to quiver and shake until it jarred a slight crack around the frame. It proceeded to tremble violently, twisting on its hinges until it abruptly flew open.

"It seems kind of anxious for you to leave."

"That's an invitation you best not refuse," Herc added.

Tony didn't need prompting. He was halfway down the sidewalk when the distant police sirens first became audible. He gunned the truck out of the drive, spun around onto the street. A trail of smoking rubber followed him around the corner of the first cross street.

Herc put his arm around Early May as they stood on the porch watching Tony speed away. The sirens grew louder.

"Is there something you'd like to tell me?" Herc suggested as Early May looked up into his baffled eyes.

"There is so much I don't know where to start. I suspect the police are headed here. When we get rid of them I'll tell you everything."

Early May slipped her hand behind his head and gently pulled it downward until their lips touched, then melded into the magical blending of motion that unifies lovers. Instead of bells they heard Elvis singing.

"It's now or never
Come hold me tight
Kiss me my darling
Be mine tonight...

The police pulled into the driveway just as their lips parted.

Chapter Thirty-one

Miss Maple held tightly to the hands on each side of her as she continued praying. Her eyes shut taut together, energy focused into the heavenly petition.

Posey kept repeating a kind of SOS mantra in her head. Please send help!

Kat endeavored to keep her vision of Elvis surrounded with love amid a vaporous cloud of white light. She managed to retain the image for a few minutes before falling into a dream-filled sleep.

Elvis joined her.

"I'm glad I caught you napping."

"I am not napping. I'm doing my part to surround you with protective white light. I'm also very busy sending you love."

"We can do better than that." Elvis' arms reached out and gathered her to him. The tender gesture and strange nature of her response surprised Kat. It seemed to encompass the very essence of her soul. All the love she had ever known distilled into the rapture of the moment coupled with a mystical feeling of serenity. The sensation that swept over her was stronger and more intense than any orgasm and completely asexual. It was deeper than the deepest stillness. Immersed in the glowing current that flowed through her being, Kat felt herself separating, floating up beyond all boundaries toward a shimmering, compelling light. The radiant manifestation filled her with infinite love. Transported, Kat became part of the intricate Truth that connects all to Oneness.

Elvis's voice seemed to echo through a distance. "You've been blessed with grace from Heaven. Remember, love is always the answer, no matter the question." His voice faded into the music nearing from all directions. Softly it emerged with words of an old song.

Love lifts me up where I belong...

On a mountain high... in a valley low

Love lifts me up where I belong....

The persistent ringing of the telephone shattered the sacred silence that had enveloped the women. Miss Maple abruptly dropped their hands as she rose from the sofa and hurried toward it.

"Maple Melton Realty," she answered out of habit. "Oh my dear, I'm so happy to hear your voice. We've been so worried. Are you injured?"

"That's got to be Early May," Posey concluded. Still dazed, Kat managed to nod her head in agreement.

Miss Maple continued to listen for a few moments. Finally she sighed, "Well that's a blessing... "Yes, that will be fine. We're so anxious to hear about your ordeal. Do take care." Miss Maple hung up the telephone. "Early May is borrowing her brother's car. She should be here in a short while."

"Is Elvis with her?" Kat asked anxiously.

"Early May indicated he had been quite helpful. Apparently he contributed some confusion to the happenings at her house."

"Confusion seems to be his specialty," Posey retorted.

"I'm just delighted our support appears to have helped him gain strength."

"Is he coming back with them or has he disappeared again?" Kat asked.

A silent wind from indiscernible directions emerged as an incandescent funnel cloud in the middle of the room. Elvis's voice preceded his emergence from the luminous vapor.

"No sense taking the long way back when I can spend the time enjoying you ladies' company. Besides Kat, you had already conjured me up. It was easy to just slip into that apparition." His silhouette briefly emanated through the mist until he materialized looking exactly as he had in Kat's dream. The same way he'd appeared that first time on the beach. White dress shirt, sleeves rolled a couple of turns, collar standing up in the back. Black slacks. No shoes.

Kat sensed he had come to say goodbye.

"It's over, isn't it?" she asked reluctantly.

"Nothing is ever truly over," Elvis answered tenderly.

"That is not what I want to hear," Posey protested as she rose quickly from the sofa. "Please tell me you are speaking in broad metaphysical terms and that our mission in Memphis is completed. I don't think I'd enjoy any more tourist time here."

Elvis smiled mischievously. "Why Posey, I'm all shook up that you're tired of my company and that you obviously haven't been enjoying your stay in my hometown."

"You know very well what I'm talking about," Posey answered curtly. "What is the current status of our situation?"

"I think it's time you all found out. We need to take a little drive," Elvis answered.

"Is there sufficient time for us to return before Early May arrives?" Miss Maple fretted.

"Early May is meeting us there."

Chapter Thirty-two

Early May knew exactly where they were going but she couldn't imagine why. Elvis's instructions had been brief. Herc hadn't needed any encouragement to come with her. He insisted on driving so that she could rest. She smiled, taking in his strong, virile profile and broad, muscular shoulders. What a lover he had proved to be. Extraordinarily sweet and gentle, belying the strength of his enormous dimensions. She reached for his hand, brought it to her lips briefly.

In return, Herc lifted her hand, brushed it with the tip of his tongue. "You're going to have to keep me going in the right direction."

"Don't worry about that. I've got my eyes on you. I'll keep you on course."

"You sure I'm talking about this drive?"

"You sure I am?"

They exchanged affectionate smiles. Early May shook her head briefly before she spoke. "At this point, I'm not sure about anything. Thank goodness we're almost there. Maybe we'll finally have some answers."

She began to search the rural road for familiar signs. Finally, in the distance she spotted a small pond behind the remains of a graying wood rail fence.

"You'll make a right turn the next time you can. The entrance to the farm is about a mile further up."

Just as they approached the edge of the fenced area, a maroon Lincoln Town car swiftly drove passed on the road where they were to turn.

"That's Kat's car. Elvis must have made it back to them."

The car quickly disappeared traveling at a high speed down the gravel road.

"I wonder what the hurry is?" Herc asked as he turned to follow them. "Think we should pick up the pace?"

"On this gravel, I think she should slow down. We'll be there in a couple of minutes any way."

They were temporarily engulfed in the dust created by the preceding vehicle. As the air cleared it was easy to spot the entrance to Belle's Breeding Barn. The metal letters sprawled in an arch over the driveway. A few yards behind it stood a huge red wooden structure with the same name painted in bold, black letters along the side. A half dozen horses were scattered around the corral next to it, munching hay. A huge fire truck dominated the parking area. Kat's car was parked on the far right side next to a couple of pickups. A black limousine took up several spaces on the left. Tony's silver truck, with the crumpled front, was closest to the entrance.

"Doc Belle sure wasn't shy about what he was doing out here," Herc observed.

"Breeding was a big part of his practice. At one time he had more champion Tennessee Walker studs than anyone in the state. I wonder what's going on with the fire truck?"

"Yeah, nothing seems to be burning outside," Herc answered as he pulled next to the Town Car.

Kat opened her door and stepped out just as they stopped. "Do you know what's happening?" she called.

"Elvis said we'd find out once we got here," Early May answered. She stepped out of the car and immediately began scanning the area. "He isn't with you?"

Kat shook her head. She was about to speak when Posey emerged from the passenger side. "You look surprisingly well considering your recent adventure." she observed.

Herc rose from the driver's side to look over the car roof at Posey. "Most of her hurt is internal. She just don't show her pain."

"What a big girl!" Posey teased.

"If someone would assist me, I'd like to stretch my legs," Miss Maple called from the back window. Herc hurried to help her.

They were standing around the two cars when firemen began to exit the building. Kat was nearest to them as they loaded their equipment. She approached the closest man. "Where was the fire located? There doesn't seem to be any outward signs."

He scrutinized her for a moment before answering. "This fire is on private property."

"We've got horses stabled here." Posey interjected. "We just came to check on them."

His demeanor softened. "The fire wasn't near the stables. It was located in the lab. There appears to have been a lightning strike in the aftermath of the storm that passed through here."

"You mean it's just now catching on fire?" Kat added in her most innocent voice. "I don't understand."

"It first hit the generator and fried the wiring in the refrigeration wall. It must have been smoldering for a time before it actually flamed. There are some real mad people in there. Seems the refrigeration has been off long enough to thaw what was frozen. Some kind of horse sperm bank. They're going to make some test it to see if any of it survived." He abruptly returned to adjusting the equipment on the truck.

"Now you can see why I wasn't worried." Elvis was sitting on the roof of Kat's car.

"Why didn't you tell us this before?" Kat asked impatiently.

"I had to make sure the refrigerator was defrosted long enough to remedy my mistake."

"And your mistake is now thawed and inactive?" Posey inquired.

Elvis laughed. "It'd be just a wet place on the sheets."

"What happened to the black box?" Early May asked.

Elvis shook his head while chuckling. "Somebody got the bright idea to try and open it with a blow torch. Ashes to ashes."

Shouting from the direction of the barn caught their attention. A short stocky man walked briskly toward the limousine. He was immaculately dress in a dark, tailored suit, black Stetson hat and ebony eel skin boots. The chauffeur hurried to open the back door for him. Just as the limo door shut, a familiar pair of large men appeared from inside. A frightened smaller man was sandwiched between them. Herc recognized his cousin immediately and started walking toward them.

"What the hell's going on?" he shouted over the mayhem.

"Don't get involved with this. It's none of your never mind. What are you doin' here anyway?" Ernie asked.

Herc ignored the question.

The second man was Tony. "I see you made it back all right," Herc observed.

"You best follow Ernie's advice and keep your nose wiped," Tony snarled. The man in the middle began to whimper.

"Call the police. I'm Dr. Todd Ledbetter. This is a kidnapping!" He pleaded as his suspended body haplessly twisted in a futile effort to get free.

"Like I said. Don't mix in this," Tony snapped. "We're just goin' a conduct some business. The Boss is about to get himself a nice little farm."

Herc threw up his hands. "Hey, I got no use for anybody who don't pay their depts. I was just wondering about all the commotion. What's with the fire truck?"

Ernie chuckled. "Weren't much of a fire. Just some wires and the fuse box. Pretty costly though. Made a mess in the freezer. Them studs got some more jerking off to do."

"Shut your mouthing. We've got to git," Tony snarled. The black limousine's motor revved in agreement.

Herc turned toward Tony. "You get your money all right?"

"Yeah, I got it. But I'm not sure that makes us even." Tony's confidence improved with the presence of backup.

Herc smiled. "Sure we're even. You wouldn't want to start something you'd be sorry for. Remember I got Early May on my side."

The horn honked a command as the black limo pulled out onto the adjoining road. Tony jerked the now subdued, dejected doctor toward the battered silver truck. Ernie immediately joined in the effort. They lifted the overpowered doctor up and into the truck's cab. Ernie slid in beside him as Tony hustled around, jumped in and started the engine.

"See you at Ma's," Ernie called as they drove away.

Elvis watched the exodus from his vantage on the roof of the car. When the dust and gravel settled, Herc started back toward the group.

At that moment Elvis stood up. "Ladies, let's adjourn to a more comfortable setting. Ms. Maple, may I impose on you one last time?"

"You're never an imposition, dear boy. I was about to suggest a return to my home might be a more agreeable setting for any further discussion."

"You're a darling. I'll meet you all there. Drive careful now," Elvis suggested as his image faded.

Chapter Thirty-three

Kat's Lincoln reached Miss Maple's well ahead of the others.

"Did it ever occur to you that everyone might not like to live as dangerously as you?" Posey asked Kat as she helped the slightly trembling elderly lady from the back seat.

"What on earth are you talking about?" Kat answered, genuinely perplexed.

"Sometimes you drive like a desperado. Like you're being pursued by the border patrol."

Miss Maple quickly intervened. "I suggest we take advantage of our extra time to prepare some refreshments." She started up the front steps.

"You don't have to ride with me," Kat snapped while exiting the car.

"If I didn't have such a fatalistic point of view, I wouldn't."

"Come girls. Let's hurry with the preparation. This has been a trying time for us all. A cup of herbal tea will be a soothing treat and I still have some of those delicious coconut cookies," Miss Maple called from the porch.

"Don't you have anything stronger? I'm afraid chamomile won't do it for me. I need an infusion of something alcoholic," Posey protested.

"I believe there is a bottle of Port or Sherry in the cupboard. And possibly some brandy."

"Let's go see how much fortification we have on hand. You might have to make a booze run before our guest arrives," Posey suggested to Kat.

"I notice a big liquor store a couple of blocks from here. I'm kind of in a wine drinking mood myself and Herc doesn't appear to be a tea sipper."

"Beer would be my first guess," Posey suggested.

Kat nodded in agreement before she ducked back inside the car. "I'll be back before you can miss me," she shouted as she backed out of the driveway. She had just cleared the entrance and was turning when Early May and Herc came up the street. She waved a greeting before speeding off.

True to her word, Kat seemed barely gone before she returned with a six pack of beer and two bottles of white wine. Everyone was sitting around the kitchen table except Miss Maple, who was standing by the cabinet next to the stove. She noticed Kat coming through the door just as she turned.

"It seems that I'm the only one who wants to partake of the tea, my dear. It was lovely of you to go after more suitable refreshments."

Herc instinctively rose to help Kat. She didn't object when he took the brown bags from her arms and placed them on the counter.

"They didn't have much of a chilled wine selection. Basically I just looked in their refrigerator for something white with a real cork in it. There is a cheap corkscrew sticking in one of the wine sacks. Naturally, there was the usual variety of beer. You look like a Miller kind of guy. Hope I guessed right," Kat smiled at Herc.

"I'm not particular when it comes to beer. Which do you want Early May?"

"Beer's fine," Early May lovingly murmured the words.

"Unless he's hovering in another part of the house, it looks like I beat Elvis back. Might as well fortify ourselves. What glasses do you want to use, Miss Maple?"

"I have some lovely ones in the china cabinet but they may need to be rinsed. And please bring three. It seems I'm not much in a chamomile mood either."

Kat smiled as she entered the dining room to retrieve the glasses. She was going to miss Miss Maple. The original feeling of affinity had deepened into a genuine affection that seemed to unite them from some long ago relationship. She sensed that Posey felt the mysterious bond. Perhaps the three of them shared a close kinship in another life?

"Need some help?" Posey asked from the doorway. She gave Kat a quizzical look as she walked toward her.

"You look almost teary eyed. You sad to be parting company with the King? That is, if he hasn't already passed on to other realms."

"He wouldn't go without a good-bye."

"With his penchant for the unpredictable, I'm not sure what he'd do."

An hour later, Kat wasn't so sure either.

Chapter Thirty-four

"Well, this is the last round unless I make another run to the store." Kat poured the final contents of the second wine bottle into Posey's outstretched glass.

"Why don't we adjourn to the living room? I'm sure we'll be more comfortable. These kitchen chairs aren't built for prolong sitting. Apparently Elvis has been detained."

Miss Maple headed for the living room. She immediately selected a large, overstuffed pink velvet chair with a matching ottoman. She adjusted the position of the footrest, then settled in the chair and elevated her feet. Herc helped a limping Early May onto the sofa. He took the seat beside her.

"I'm going to get that rocking chair off the porch, if it's all right with you Miss Maple?" Kat asked.

"Certainly, dear. I find the motion very soothing."

"I think better when I rock. It calms my mind."

"I'm for anything that will do that. I'll help you drag it in here," Posey offered.

"You ladies have been too long without a man around." Herc rose from the sofa. "No need to put yourself out as long as I'm here. Just hold the door open."

Minutes later they were all seated, waiting with a quiet sense of expectation. As if on cue, a faint whirring sound engulfed the room accompanied by confetti-sized shining sprinkles floating through the atmosphere. Immediately, a current of air began to circle, gathering the shimmering pieces into a dazzling silver funnel of illumination that glistened like sunbeams dancing on a field of early morning frost. The tiny crystals spiraled faster and faster until a form began to develop in it's interior. The spinning outer area grew smaller as the center enlarged, shape shifting into the familiar caped figure. Elvis emerged, clad in a new rhinestone studded white jumpsuit. The cape over his shoulders was a marvel of the purest, softest, white feathers with a halo of shimmering light surrounding each one.

Kat stopped the chair and her breath in mid rock. Elvis had never looked more majestically heaven sent. Her voice trembled as she spoke. "We were beginning to think you'd gone without saying good-bye."

"Now darlin', you know I'd never do that. I was just making sure that Dr. Todd didn't have to pay more than he should. Losing his farm and all the potential stud fees seemed payment enough."

Early May shifted uncomfortably on the sofa while alternately rubbing her aching wrists. "I was kind of hoping you had to convince Tony."

"He did seem inclined to inflict a little more damage than was necessary. However, it didn't take much to persuade him. A little prod here and there. Some unidentifiable noise.

A few of the vials unexpectedly shattering on the floor. I think our last encounter made him a bit jumpy. He had leaving on his mind before the final papers were signed."

"Is the voltage from that outfit giving you some vitality or have you managed to pull yourself together?" Posey asked.

"I stopped by Graceland. The prayers at the Memorial Garden always infuse me with such joy and strength. I wanted to look good for our farewell."

"So we've come to the end of our time together," Miss Maple stated sadly.

"There's never an end. Just a temporary pause, so to speak. Our worlds are never far apart."

"I'm sure mine is ever nearer yours."

"I'll be waiting when its time for you to cross. It's a beautiful period of reunion. Every life that's touched ours with love gathers for the welcoming. The celebration is beyond mortal imagination."

"Will you be there for me?" Kat asked earnestly.

"Darlin', you know I will."

"What about the rest of us?" Early May asked.

"I'm there for anyone that calls out to me."

"And in this life? Anymore appearances planned?" Posey questioned.

"Posey, love, I didn't plan this one."

"So if we really need you, will you be able to come back?" Kat asked hesitantly

"Define really need...no, no, I'm just kidding. You know that I'm never further than a dream away."

"I believe she's referring to a visit during our waking hours," Posey added.

"The future is a series of choices. The road we travel depends entirely on the paths we choose. Your fate in each life is determined that way."

"You didn't answer my question," Posey persisted.

"I answered it." Elvis smiled as he glanced around the group.

"Can't you afford us any further insights?" Miss Maple pleaded

"Maybe a glimpse at the meaning of life," Kat added, half in jest.

"The other side is as thin as smoke and as easy to penetrate. The main lesson of each incarnation is that love is everything. Start by loving yourselves as the most special person you will ever love, because your body is God's creation. A divine gift essential to your completeness. That's why YOU are your number one priority."

"That sounds incredibly selfish," Early May reflected.

"Not when you experience love without ego. When you love from your spirit. Making yourself a loving, forgiving person should be your journey."

"Or we end up in Hell?" Posey asked sardonically.

Elvis laughed. "Hell is pretty much what you believe it to be. At least at the beginning when we first cross over and refuse to see the reality."

"So if you don't believe in Hell there won't be one?" Posey continued.

"Oh there's a kind of scoreboard that keeps track. It's not judgmental. More of a measuring device to determine how much love you've given the world. You see it and all your life's experiences with heartbreaking clarity at death." Elvis paused then chuckled. "It sure makes you feel like hell."

Elvis' eyes briefly lingered on each person in the room. "Now it's time to drift on. I give my love gratefully to each of you for all your help." He turned and gave Kat the force of his full attention.

"Kat, darlin', you are my special earth angel. Bless you for your faith in things seen and unseen. I will never forget your devotion." Elvis gathered his lips in the shape of a kiss then blew softly in her direction. Kat felt a tingle surge through her body.

Elvis smiled as he raised his arms dramatically, lifting the resplendent feather cape. His image intensified with a shimmering inner light that emanated through all the cells of his body. The cape promptly amplified into a pair of tremendous golden-tinged wings that lifted him upward toward a beckoning luminous circle in the ceiling.

His laughter filled the room.

"Can't wait to see my encore!"

Biography

Cherry Cooper McKenzie was born on her mother's birthday on September 15th, 1936, in Memphis, Tennessee. She attended a variety of schools until finally transferring from South Side to Humes High School the second semester of her sophomore year. She and Elvis sat by each other in Miss Helen Lockries' Speech and Drama Class. He invited her to the junior/senior prom that year. Cherry now lives in Irving, Texas with her dog Annie. She has three married daughters and a granddaughter.

Cherry and Elvis
Humes Prom 1952

Barbara Weatherly Rice (leftside) and prom group

Printed in the United States
145741LV00010B/3/A